THE GOODLIEST LAND

THE GOODLIEST LAND: NORTH CAROLINA

Text by Nancy Roberts

Photographs by Bruce Roberts

Doubleday & Company, Inc.

Garden City, New York, 1973

ISBN 0-385-04302-3
Library of Congress Catalog Card Number 72-89345

Book design by M. F. Gazze

To Charles Rado
A Frenchman by birth,
an American by choice,
a Carolinian in spirit

Contents

THE GOODLIEST LAND

The Goodliest Land

"We have discovered the maine to be the goodliest land
under the cope of heaven . . ."
—Ralph Lane, September 3, 1585

North Carolina is as much a state of mind as it is a state of the Union. Those who have grown up within its borders and left for other sections of the country still love their state passionately and long for the day when they can return. People who discover North Carolina by moving here from other places put down roots gratefully into the fertile land of eastern North Carolina, the rolling hills of the Piedmont, the rugged mountain country or succumb happily to the way of life of the coast. These adopted sons and daughters become Carolinians as ardent as the native born, convinced that they, too, have "come home."

The story goes that God made North Carolina first so that he might practice on mountains, plains, rivers and seashores; then, following it as a model, shaped the rest of the country.

North Carolina is a diverse land, one of sharp contrast and surprises, of regions that have little in common—the qualities of its people are often as unexpected as the contours of the state. North Carolina stretches 503 miles from east to west and runs 188 miles from north to south at its greatest length. The "Old North State" was one of the original thirteen states and it has seen a long and colorful history—wars with the Indians, harassment by pirates, crucial Revolutionary battles, the greatest land invasion until D-Day, which occurred at Fort Fisher, the last major battle of the Civil War, and fully as important, the oldest state university in the country.

In the early years, western North Carolina was much isolated from the rest of the state. Now it has many good roads, and recently a highway was completed linking the mountains and the coast. Today remote mountaineers, sophisticated urbanites from the

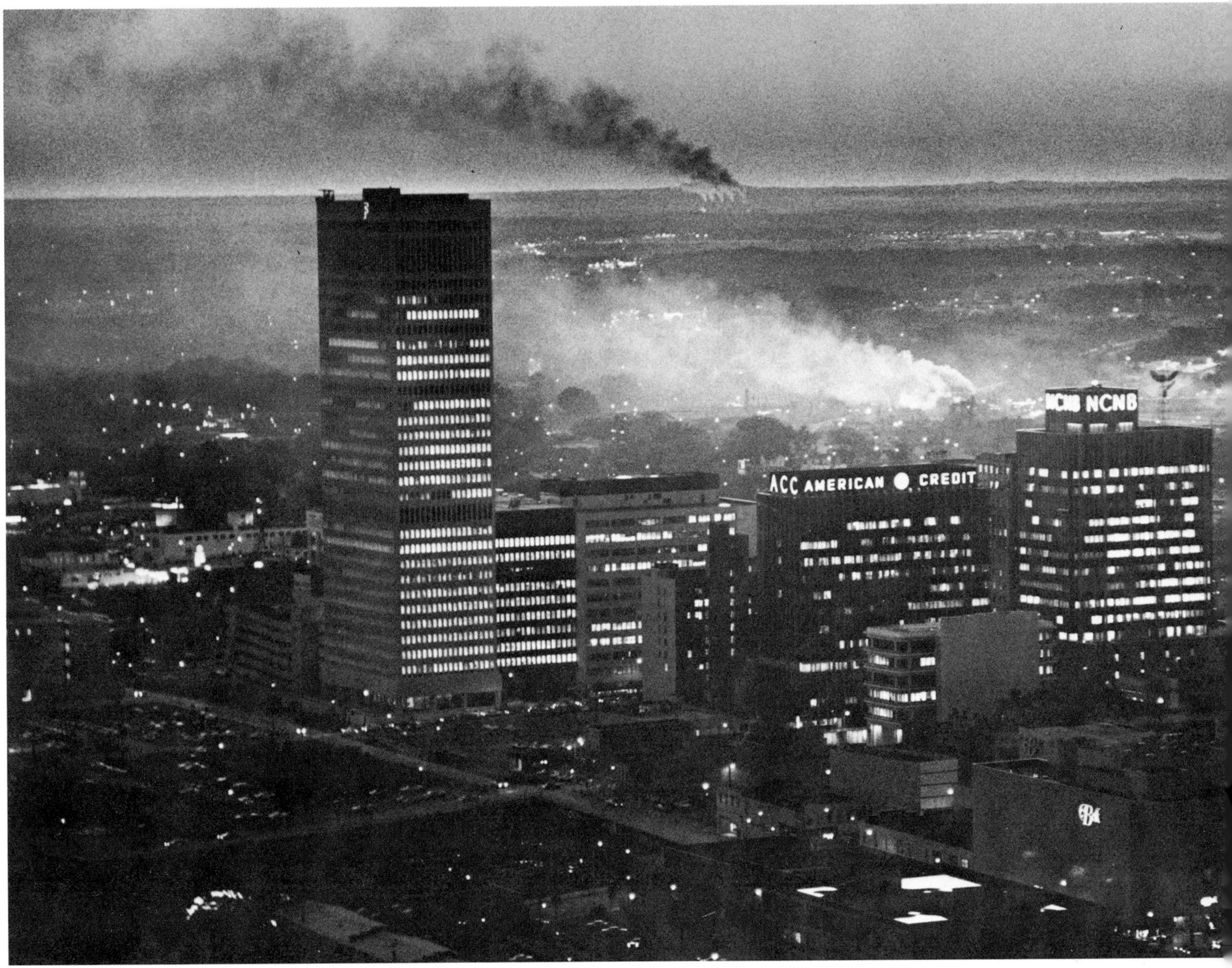
NCNB NCNB
ACC AMERICAN CREDIT

Piedmont or Research Triangle and coastal fishermen can have a look at each other; whether they have much to say is another matter.

Mountaineers with fierce loyalties to family and land, Outer Bankers and coastal folk content to live to themselves and wrest their livelihood from the sea, eastern Carolina farmers, often judged provincial by city standards, but firmly grounded in religious principles and the art of politics, sometimes baffle the more transient, corporation-oriented residents of the Piedmont who seek culture and progress as they struggle with the full spectrum of urban problems.

Outside of the Piedmont and cities near the more heavily industrialized Research Triangle area, there is sectionalism and a strong sense of self-identity. Attitude and decision-making processes have not been influenced by what is good for the corporation or group pressures. In a state still slightly more rural than urban, the farmer and small businessman are individualistic, making their decisions and setting their goals in a manner both unpredictable and unmanageable by that combination of bureaucracy and scientific method termed "bureautechnocracy."

Rural representatives still exercise a considerable degree of power in the legislature. They cling tenaciously to a less hectic pace of life and, thus far, have refused to gear themselves to ever-increasing industrial productivity as an ultimate value. Since traditional ideas concerning basic needs are strongly ingrained, they are not easily influenced product consumers. But how long they will continue to provide a balance is questionable, for each census shows an increasing number moving from small farms to the cities, and as they become urbanized traditional values will be more subject to change.

The lights come on at dusk in Charlotte's offices and buildings. The National Geographic *called North Carolina "The Dixie Dynamo" and this picture shows the heart of it. Charlotte and its suburbs are now close to a half million in population and some city officials have predicted the figure will double in the next ten years.*

The Outer Banks Beckon

Climb the sand dunes, feel the wind—the same wind that lofted the Wright Brothers' glider and later their plane, supporting the fragile craft a few feet above the earth in proof that man could fly. A wind forever blowing, shifting the dunes, changing the shapes of inlets and whistling through the telegraph wires that span the marshes. Two score years later it raised the wings of Colonel Billy Mitchell's planes which, rising, circled Cape Hatteras and bombed two obsolete battleships moored offshore. The ships sunk, perhaps a foretaste of Pearl Harbor. The planes flew away, and now the sea gulls soar upon the wind alone with such grace that it is surprising man had to make noisy engines do what the gulls do so effortlessly.

The wind, not man, owns this string of sandy islands from the Virginia line to below Cape Lookout. For the wind built them, carrying the sand, bringing the seeds of plants, blowing rain clouds to water them. On the wind rides the savage, battering force of the winter storms strong enough to slice an island asunder as the 1962 hurricane did to Hatteras. An invisible architect designing, moving, building and sometimes tearing down. But this long strip of barrier islands is in many places still the wild and lonely beach Sir Francis Drake saw in 1586 when he anchored his ships off Roanoke Island. The openness and natural beauty have been preserved by the Cape Hatteras National Seashore Park, and now Cape Lookout National Seashore has been added to the southernmost half of the chain. It was none too soon, for this two-hundred-mile stretch of ocean frontage would surely have been subdivided and commercialized if the state of North Carolina and the Park Service had not acted.

From Whalebone Junction at the southern boundary of Nags Head, the National Seashore encompasses seventy miles of windswept barrier islands that flex southward into the Atlantic to the point of Cape Hatteras, then arch back to follow the mainland. The Cape Hatteras National Seashore is divided into three sections—Bodie Island, Hatteras Island and Ocracoke Island—each separated from the other by an inlet.

Looking at the great sand dunes the wind has built around Kitty Hawk, Kill Devil Hills and Nags Head it is hard to realize that in 1524 the explorer Verrazano found this land covered with tall trees and lush vegetation. It was so beautiful that he called it "Arcadia" after Vergil's concept of the ideal landscape inhabited by simple, virtuous people. At Kitty Hawk a monument marks the site of the Wright Brothers' flight—a success that has enabled us to get places faster but see less. A few miles southward a short detour swings by Roanoke Island, site of Sir Walter Raleigh's Lost Colony of 1585–87, one of the unsolvable mysteries of history.

Standing on the shores of Cape Hatteras, one is not far from the spot where two great rivers of the sea, the warm waters of the indigo-blue Gulf Stream and the icy gray waters of the Labrador Current meet in a dramatic, head-on clash of foam and fury. Beneath these waves are the immense underwater sand dunes of Diamond Shoals —the graveyard of the Atlantic—stretching out into the ocean for twelve miles and bringing disaster to ships who stray too close to them. Islanders staring out to sea where the two currents meet decide whether or not to put out their nets by the color of the water. The Gulf Stream is clear, but the Labrador Current often carries enough sand to tinge the water. If it is a dirty color the fishermen don't venture out, for the catch will be a slim one.

The waves' enormous strength sucks the sand back into the sea with such force that sometimes the dark, gaunt frame of a shipwreck many years old is disrobed by the deep. Curved ribs of an old schooner jut skyward and mammoth timbers pierced by rusted bolts rest upon the sand, arousing romantic speculations about men who sailed their last voyage in this doomed ship. One of the most eerie stories is that of the ghost ship of Ocracoke Island. On a stormy winter night in 1921, the five-masted *Carroll A. Deering* was driven high up on Diamond Shoals. At dawn there sat the stranded schooner with sails set as if she had been abandoned in a hurry, the seas boiling white around her. The ocean remained so rough that it was several days before she could be boarded and by then her seams were beginning to rip apart. On the ship there were no signs of a struggle, food was still in the galley pots, but there was no trace of captain or crew. The only living creature on board was the ship's cat. Since the vessel could not be floated, there was nothing left but to dynamite her. She did not remain where she was sunk. Later the bow drifted like some spectral ship westerly through the water

Cape Hatteras Lighthouse. Overleaf

until it came ashore on Ocracoke Island, where it was buried in a shroud of drifting sand. But sometimes after a winter storm the wreck of the *Carroll A. Deering* emerges once more along the shoreline to be seen for a while before the wind covers it over with sand again.

The Pea Island Wild Life Refuge on Hatteras is a haven for both birds and bird watchers—the winter home of thousands of snow geese, Canada geese, ducks and the whistling swan. Here, too, come herons, loons, bald eagles and many other unusual species of birds including the nesting gadwall, which is very choosy about where it nests. Those who like to walk long expanses of desolate beach and enjoy isolation will find the Banks most desirable in spring and fall. Not everyone will feel comfortable on the empty infinite sweep of beach, but for some it is an exhilarating, restoring experience. Neon signs are left far behind, for sixty-mile-long Hatteras is owned largely by the Park Service except for a few scattered villages where there are a number of motels. The Park Service provides camp sites, and those seeking more luxurious accommodations will find them, along with delicious seafood, outside its boundaries at the motels and restaurants of Kitty Hawk, Nags Head, Manteo, Beaufort and Morehead City.

Leaving Hatteras, a free ferry operated by the state takes over transporting cars to the remaining populated island of Ocracoke, a picturesque fishing village, whose people enjoy their isolation from the mainland. This small island with its tall massive lighthouse was a favorite rendezvous of the daring, ruthless pirate Blackbeard, and there are those who think his treasure may still be buried somewhere on the island.

There are encouraging signs that the residents of the coastal counties are concerned about preserving their natural resources and the delicate ecological balance of the Banks.

Carl Sandburg wrote, "Save the dunes. They belong to the people. They represent the signature of time and eternity. Their loss would be irrevocable." May we forever keep the Outer Banks a place cherished by man, continuing to bring forth "mornings when men are new-born."

Surf Fishing Is Their Heritage

"I have looked at the sea a thousand times from the same spot and I have seen a thousand different seas," says author David Stick, who lives at Kitty Hawk.

Some things change and some do not, but for surf-fishing crews, like the one captained by Lee Peele of Hatteras, it's a mixture. They fish the same cold waters and tossing surf their fathers and grandfathers fished before them—lonely expanses of beach stretching from Oregon Inlet to Ocracoke. But brawny arms with gloved hands no longer are the only means of hauling in the long nets. Now, they are pulled in to shore by sleek pickup trucks.

It is a wintertime means of livelihood few tourists ever see. In the summer these same hardy net fishermen may be somewhere else, tending their crab pots, fishing from boats in the sound or offshore. But with the change of season comes a change in the ways of the fishermen. For with the gusty cold winds and churning waters come the big striped bass and blues swarming in the surf for the taking.

Often as many as four crews will work the surf and everyone seems to be named Midgett, Burrus, Gray or Scarborough, descendants of families who for generations have lived and died beside the sea.

"In one crew every man was named Midgett, but nobody claimed kin to anyone else," says Ray Couch who lives at Hatteras and watches the fishermen almost daily.

A crew usually consists of four men, a mile-long net and a pickup truck pulling a trailer with a small boat perched upon it. Launching the boat at one of the inlets, the net is played out through the shimmering water in a gigantic, arching crescent until it is finally brought back to shore through the breakers. Like a precision race team changing tires at a pit stop, the pickup truck driver zooms down the beach until his front tires rest in the foam of a receding wave. Quickly the members of the crew attach a hook to the net and with a shift of the gears the truck backs away from the water a hundred yards, pulling the net in with it.

These men who fish the frothy white surf with nets are descendants of the same men who manned the lifeboat stations that in years past dotted the beach every eight or ten miles. It was their fathers and grandfathers who pushed small lifeboats fearlessly through the breakers and rescued many a life from the raging seas. In the days before the Coast Guard these men were called the Life Saving Service and they were a proud and hardy lot.

It is incongruous, yet typical of the Outer Banks and this unchanging breed of men that they would still be wresting their livelihood from the sea, but hauling it in with a modern pickup truck. Yet, why not? For these are a practical people doing what they know best, and who would expect them to do it the hard way when a truck could accomplish their goal more quickly and easily.

Nothing is ever wasted here. The people find a use for everything, just as they did long years ago when a half-drowned schoolteacher clinging to a plank washed up during a storm. They simply dried him out, built a one-room school and put him to work. They had been thinking about a school and a teacher was provided. He stayed on, marrying one of the local girls, who are noted for their beauty.

Standing in the bright sunlight on a January morning watching the fishing crews at work, one almost forgets that just out of sight are the remains of hundreds of unfortunate vessels fallen victim to the treacherous shoals, and not so very long ago the ancestors of these fishermen were hauling shipwrecked human beings to safety through perilous waters. Written into the terms of the Cape Hatteras National Seashore Park is the agreement that the descendants of the Life Saving Crews forever have the right to cast their nets into the surf, and for them the sea will always remain their challenge and their livelihood.

With its net out, this trawler moves slowly in the hazy dawn.

The Chowan County Court House built in 1767 is perhaps the finest Georgian courthouse in the South. The cupola was sometimes illuminated during great celebrations as it was when North Carolina ratified the Constitution.

North Carolina's Living Williamsburg

Crossing the broad, blue Chowan River on Highway 17 leading to Edenton is to enter a living Williamsburg. The people with their twentieth-century clothes appear almost out of place as they walk streets lined with beautifully preserved colonial homes and buildings still in use. Edenton was the seat of government of the young colony of Carolina for many years—the county around it called Chowan, after the river and the Chowanook Indians who inhabited the area.

"Here was a good country where crops were heavier, forests deeper and trees taller. In the spring the herring and greater fish also swam up in schools to spawn." Drained by small creeks of sweet, black water, the large, awe-inspiring swamps of cypress and hardwoods were full of an amazing variety of plant and bird life. At the water's edge where the blue Chowan and the Albemarle Sound meet and blend lies the town. This Albemarle section of North Carolina was the earliest settled and for nearly a century it was "the cradle of the colony," the home of educated, ambitious men who were to play a vital part in the political future of the young state and nation.

Today, Edenton seems delightfully remote from the problems of the world. Black and white youngsters fish together on the waterfront. Merchants and townspeople maintain a leisurely pace of life.

The beautiful old Chowan County Court House, built to serve the needs of the area in 1767, continues to hear cases and its windows still look out over the long, terraced green lawn toward the sound. Afternoon sunlight warms the rich tones of the handmade bricks and casts shadows on the worn rock slab steps brought to this marsh-like coastal region from England. Within the courthouse a sharp pointed picket fence with a gate in the center stretches across the back of the courtroom—a deterrent, if not a barrier, to the criminal who would consider a break for freedom.

Outdoors, children play on the courthouse lawn, running up the steps of the terraces, chasing each other or, as one mother put it, "shine cutting on the grass."

The clerk of court and registrar of deeds occupy the same offices as their predecessors two centuries ago. Judges have sat and lawyers have spoken in this courtroom at left, while Washington, Jefferson, Lincoln, Roosevelt, Nixon and every one of our Presidents has been in office.

Near Hertford on a small promontory of land called Durant's Neck is the Leigh Mansion (shown at right), built by Colonel James Leigh about 1825. The house is one of the most beautiful of many interesting plantation homes in the Hertford area.

Thank You, Earl of Hertford

North of Edenton a picturesque S-shaped bridge, spanning the Perquimans River, forms the approach to the small town of Hertford. The view from the bridge of the moon rising over the river is thought to have inspired the writers of the song "Carolina Moon." Hertford is a sequestered, quiet village, undiscovered by the average tourist who speeds past on the U. S. 17 bypass, but this community and the countryside around it make for a fascinating trip into the past.

The Earl of Hertford planned the town in typically British symmetrical fashion in 1758 and named it after the borough of Hertford in England. An old map shows carefully laid-out streets, identically sized rectangular lots and stated requirements as to the size and materials of each home. Described by an official of the North Carolina Department of Archives and History as one of "the state's most historical areas," Hertford is the home of North Carolina's first permanent settlement, first church building, and it was here that the first religious service in the province of North Carolina was held.

Its spacious white frame homes with their green lawns sloping down to the waterfront are in the path of cool summer breezes from the Perquimans River, for this land is a peninsula bounded on three sides by water. Many of the houses are still owned by the descendants of families who built them in the early 1800s. But this is no static restoration. These homes are lived in and enjoyed! Good fishing and hunting abound, for there are quail, dove, duck, goose, deer, fox, bear, coon and possum. For a time there was no doctor, but that changed after an Atlanta physician discovered Hertford's easygoing ways.

Developers vie eagerly for waterfront property along Albemarle Sound, although, over the years, successive hurricanes continue to claim some of the waterfront land the tourists buy. Somewhere out there under the lapping blue waves are the graves of the early settlers. Cracked, gray-streaked old headstones rise out of the mud on the bottom where only the unblinking eyes of an occasional fish may sometimes pause to stare at the letters.

Seventy-five years ago there were great seine fisheries in this part of eastern North Carolina and one haul of the net could mean a million herring and two or three thousand shad. The nets extended out one or two miles and were handled by steam barges to carry out the net and winches with steam power to bring them back to shore. Nearby churches would hold Sunday-school picnics at the fisheries, and everyone would feast happily on fresh fried shad and herring roe. Vans of covered carts and wagons would pass through Hertford on their way to the fisheries for a year's supply of herring, and often the catch was so large the excess fish were used to fertilize the land.

Where has all this wealth of nature's gone? It is no longer there. Perhaps so much of the fresh waters to the west have been dammed up and so many inlets to the east shoaled until the spawning grounds in the sounds and rivers were ruined—victims to "progress" too profligate to envision the destruction of ocean's gift to man.

Early land grants averaged three hundred acres, generally extending back a mile from a river or creek. As in the South Carolina low country, many handsome old plantation houses may still be seen along these rivers. Farming is now highly mechanized in this corn and peanut country, but there is something incongruous about seeing a gigantic piece of modern farm equipment in a field beside a home built over a century ago. The people of Perquimans County have raised the same crops for years—corn, peanuts and, more recently, soybeans.

Not far from the town of Hertford is the white-columned Winslow House where the Perry family now live. Set far back from the road overlooking a tremendous green lawn where sheep graze peacefully, it is a scene of pastoral beauty. Riverside Farms, as the house is more formally named, was built in the 1790s and most of the windows still contain the old panes of glass—a rainbow of colors, if glimpsed from the right angle.

"My parents lived here for years and farmed this land," says slim, young-looking Myrtle Williams Perry. "Although we didn't own this home, I was born in it. After I married, my husband and I moved out here to farm. The seclusion is natural to me and I love it. We shear the sheep and sell the wool, also the lambs. The children roam the fields and walk to the river to explore and fish." The Perquimans River is about a quarter of a mile back of the house. "This was once Indian territory and when I was a child

Penelope Barker, who later lived in this house, presided over the Edenton Tea Party, October 25, 1774. This was probably the earliest known instance of political activity on the part of women in the American colonies. Fifty-one Edenton ladies held a subversive tea party and said they would not serve tea until the tax came off. There were no unguarded British ships loaded with tea in the harbor at the time or Edenton might have become as famous as Boston. The house is now headquarters for Historic Edenton, Inc., and is also a visitor's center and museum.

my father used to find arrowheads in the fields. Our boys, Scott and Chris, like to hunt for them, too." The Perry family is unusual in modern-day America, for few children in our mobile society live on the same land where their grandfathers once lived.

Social life centers around Hertford, its schools and churches, or hunting, fishing and boating. There isn't even an X-rated movie in town because the nearest movie theater is Edenton or Elizabeth City, so most recreation takes place at the school or homes of the young people.

Unlike some towns in New England or the Northeast where families have lived for many generations, there is little suspicion of strangers or reluctance to receive them into the life of the community. A doctor moving recently from Atlanta to Hertford says, "There isn't the urgency here. People are friendly and socializing isn't as categorized." But, more than that, there is the feeling that in this region of North Carolina the atmosphere of the past still tarries, the atmosphere of "a fruitful land, ripe and waiting."

A Capital from the Woods of Wake

In 1867 a runaway apprentice came home to Raleigh, but no one bothered to callect the ten-dollar reward. The man was Andrew Johnson, President of the United States. It was two years after the close of the Civil War when "immense crowds" gathered to see him in the streets of Raleigh. The occasion was the dedication of a monument honoring the heroism of the President's father, Jacob Johnson, whose rescue of two men from drowning is said to have caused his own death from exposure.

Shortly after his arrival in the city, the President began greeting citizens in the Capitol building, and later at the cemetery he heard his father eulogized by a former governor of North Carolina. But among the crowds of citizens turning out to honor him there must have been mixed emotions, for memories of one hundred thousand federal troops marching through the streets of Raleigh could not fade quickly. These same people had stood watching stunned and silent on April 11, 1865, as General Joe Johnston's gaunt and tattered men retreated, straggling along, grim faced and worn. Youngsters in the crowd held out glasses of water to the exhausted men. It was a heartbreaking sight for the people and there was fear for the morrow as well. The treasurer was hastily gathering up money and records to carry out of the city. Governor Zebulon Vance was to spend that night and the next day at the railroad depot north of the capital, supervising the loading of one train after another with blankets, shoes, uniforms, cloth, medicine, bacon and corn. Bank presidents were rushing their funds out of the city by rail and wagon, headed hopefully toward Greensboro and Charlotte. Citizens were desperately seeking hiding places for their valuables. One family placed their entire supply of gold coins under the rocks in their garden, others hid valuables under basement floors.

Five thousand people lived in Raleigh in 1865. It was an attractive little town, beautifully laid out in the midst of the woods of Wake County. But not even the sight of flowering dogwoods nor the warm April sunlight could dispel the apprehension and

Raleigh is a county seat as well as a state capital. This impressive building takes the place of the old Wake County Courthouse.

gloom that lay like a cloud over the people. Would their city share the flaming fate of Columbia, South Carolina, or of Atlanta? At one end of Fayetteville Street stood the domed Capitol building and at the other rose the graceful classic columns of the two-story-brick governor's palace. The city overflowed with Confederate wounded. Pettigrew Hospital had not been able to house them all and many were being cared for in churches and private homes. What happens when a city goes up in flames? General Sherman with the entire Union Army behind him was on the march to Raleigh. He had left a trail of ashes and devastation throughout the South. Would this be the fate of Raleigh? All wondered.

The morning of April 13 was cloudy with a drizzling spring rain. The last of the Confederate cavalry had gone. As Sherman rode into Raleigh he found only empty streets and closed stores. Townspeople stared fearfully out between parted curtains at the general who had terrorized the South. He was a shabby man with a reddish, unkempt beard. The Union soldiers were ragged. Some carried hams and chickens or sacks of meal over their shoulders, but they were orderly and seemed to mean no harm. Sherman had given orders there was to be no plundering or looting, probably because he had been so severely criticized about Columbia. Or, perhaps, he remembered old friendships with North Carolina classmates at West Point. Yankee troops made an effort to be friendly and calm the people's fears. Hope sprang up that the city would be spared and citizens began to venture out upon the streets. The following day a note was delivered to Sherman. General Joe Johnston was ready to surrender. It was a few days after Lincoln's death but word had not reached Raleigh of the assassination.

What were the thoughts in Washington of the new President, a runaway apprentice from Raleigh who had educated himself and become President of the Union? Surely, he must have thought about the armies under his command entering the city of his birth. Did he feel any sympathy for his native state? There was little he could do, for telegraph lines were down and the country in a state of shock as it gradually learned of Lincoln's death.

The ways of men change little, and it is not surprising that Raleigh became the capital because of political influence and lobbying at a dinner party. Colonel Joel Lane, a wealthy and influential settler, offered his land to the state, but the commission selected by the legislature first voted against the Lane property. However, the decision was delayed (this is not uncommon today!), and Lane wined and dined the members at a lavish dinner. After the dinner they voted five to one to buy his site, and thus began one of probably a number of decisions in Raleigh, arrived at after good food and drink, that have influenced the course of the state's history. The Capitol building, which was soon constructed, was not a model of beauty and the small, muddy village around it was for a while so primitive that most government officials found good reasons for not living there. Other cities in the state, jealous at not being selected, made fun of the "city of streets without houses." There were the governor's mansion, two inns and a few stores and houses.

But as the trade and commerce of the area grew and the new Raleigh and Gaston Railroad was built, the town and county began to prosper.

In June of 1840 there was a three-day blast and toot for the new railroad with train excursions, fireworks, dancing, banqueting and tours of the new Capitol building. Small as Raleigh was, there were enough people interested in culture to begin the North Carolina Museum, the Raleigh Theatre and a library. For the more plebeian there were cockfights and circuses. The first State Fair in 1853 drew as many as four thousand visitors in a single day. The Fair is still an important annual event, and in secluded places at night, cockfights are secretly held, despite the fact that they are now against the law.

Christmas was widely celebrated in Raleigh homes, as elsewhere in the state, and was an occasion for visiting between kinfolk who thought nothing of coming and staying for several weeks. For the blacks, too, it was a time to celebrate. On Christmas morning there was the custom of calling out, "Christmas gif," and if it was said to the mistress of the house before she could say it, invariably it called for a gift from her. This custom is still remembered by children who grew up in the 1930s and '40s. It was not the white people alone who responded to "Christmas gif," for on Christmas morning the cook or butler often arrived with a package of homemade sausage, cracklings or some small gift which was gratefully received by the household.

It was also during the nineteenth century that the shocking treatment given the insane was uncovered by humanitarian Dorothy Dix on her tour throughout the state. Two governors had asked the legislature for better care of the insane, but the legislature had refused to act. Finally, Miss Dix received the help of a Democratic leader,

James C. Dobbin of Cumberland County, who made an eloquent plea for a hospital for the proper care and treatment of the insane. A state hospital in Raleigh, named after Miss Dix, was the result. It is time for another James C. Dobbin to rise up in the legislature and move the consciences of his fellow legislators. Once again our retarded and our mentally ill need better care, and our state institutions are sadly lacking in funds.

Along with Dorothy Dix, Carrie Nation and the automobile, the industrial revolution came to Raleigh and with it came growth to the capital city. Today Raleigh has become many things to many people. To some it is a center of commerce, to others, an educational oasis with its six colleges, for the politically inclined it is the eye of the hurricane. North Carolina State University at Raleigh, Duke University at Durham and the University of North Carolina at Chapel Hill are the points of the triangle that former Governor Luther H. Hodges saw in his mind as the Research Triangle. Now, the Triangle Park, this brain child of Hodges with its exciting research facilities is influencing Raleigh both educationally and culturally.

"Seeing Hands." The gift of enjoying art is not restricted to the sighted at North Carolina's Museum of Art in Raleigh. The Mary Biddle Duke Gallery for the Blind is toured regularly by blind students. The museum houses almost two thousand major works of art, valued in the millions, and has one of the finest collections in the country.

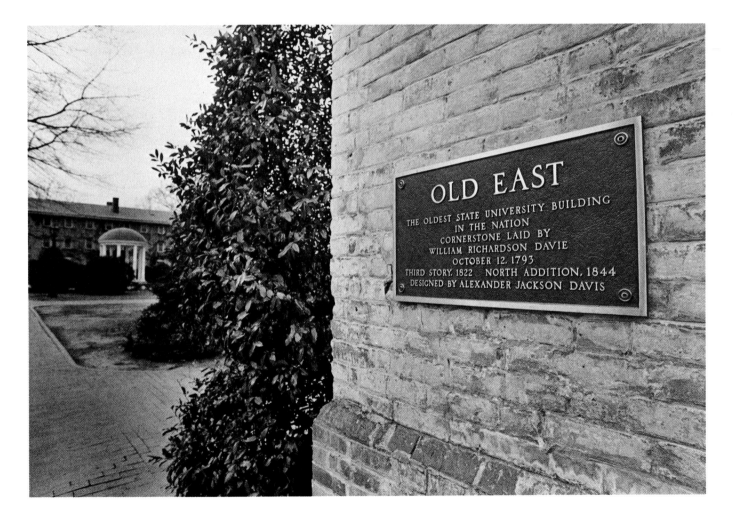

Chapel Hill—the First State University

"A granite promontory jutted out from the north and west, high above the valley. Two bold creeks at the foot of the hill were ready to turn the gristmills and sawmills of farmers and lumbermen. A profusion of springs and brooks gushed from the hillside carving the terrain into bends, glens and meadows. All this was covered with a mountainlike growth of oak, hickory, ash, laurel and rhododendron. Chapel Hill was already a beautiful place," wrote Robert House in his history of Orange County.

When the cornerstone was laid here for America's first state university in the autumn of 1793, it was the beginning of a long struggle. After the university had been open a month, one student finally arrived, having walked from Wilmington to Chapel Hill. What a humble beginning for a university that now has nineteen thousand students and a reputation for excellence throughout the world.

Although the University of North Carolina at Chapel Hill has long been a pace setter among American universities, it would be a mistake to assume that it is the only part of North Carolina's university system where exciting things in higher education are happening. It is one of sixteen institutions of higher learning in the state and is part of the new consolidated university; each college has its own unique qualities and assets. There are attractive campuses and beautiful new buildings at all of these schools, but there is only one Chapel Hill where the ancient trees still shade the central campus and brick walkways, where couples sit and talk on the limbs of the large apple trees between the classroom buildings near the library or pause to refresh themselves at the Old Well. The main street of the "village" has changed very little although the university continues to grow. Dormitories are filled to overflowing and many students live in apartments. In fact, "There are two Chapel Hills now," says author and professor Walter Spearman. "There is a whole new town growing up around Chapel Hill. The graduate school will probably increase. People come here to study, to write or to retire in a stimulating atmosphere."

The oldest state university building in the nation still stands on the campus of America's first state university, the University of North Carolina at Chapel Hill.

So, there are many Chapel Hills—in the minds of the old graduates, in the minds of the professors, in the minds of the present-day students. There is a Chapel Hill changing . . . new buildings growing up among the old . . . more students from far places, but as Wolfe preserved Asheville on the pages of his novels, forever timeless, so are the memories of Chapel Hill engraved on the mind of each student who has gone there. Its graduates—scientists, engineers, doctors, lawyers, statesmen, politicians, businessmen—are everywhere. It was the first state university in America, and it is a great university. Time passes. But Chapel Hill remains.

More buildings, more programs, more students are the harvest of academic excellence that the University of North Carolina at Chapel Hill has achieved.

Duke pep band at Atlantic Coast Conference Tournament. The ACC basketball play-offs each year are always tumultuous, bringing together the top rivals in North Carolina as well as South Carolina. The ACC includes Carolina, Duke, Wake Forest and North Carolina State in North Carolina.

The Lumbee Indians have concentrated on education. Dr. English Jones, a Lumbee Indian, is president of Pembroke State University. A major part of North Carolina's greater university system, its origin was that of an Indian college. The university grants both master's and doctor's degrees and attracts students not only from the area but from many sections of the country. Some historians believe that this tribe is partly descended from survivors of the Lost Colony because their family names in many cases are similar, and their language has characteristics in common with Elizabethan English. The Lumbees are one of North Carolina's most interesting people. They have produced bridge builders and surgeons, architects and educators—all without the help of the great white father.

Tobacco tycoon James B. Duke was one of the world's most successful merchants and empire builders. In front of the cathedral, heart of the Gothic campus of Duke University, stands the great man himself, re-created in bronze, gazing out upon his masterpiece.

The Mission of Sam Ragan

SUMMER SOUTH
Even now in September
The crepe myrtle blooms.
This land forever seeks
Summer. It holds it tightly
In its hand, and with hoarse voice
Proclaims it as its own.
The reds dominate,
Bright reds in waning green.
—Sam Ragan

Sam Ragan leans back in the chair in his office. He is dressed in a soft blue corduroy jacket and blue bow tie, and there is still the aura of pine woods and wide expanse of sky about this poet-writer, who comes from Southern Pines, the sand-hills section of North Carolina.

He is North Carolina's Secretary of Art, Culture and History, and he is described by the city editor of the capital paper (*The News and Observer*) as the amalgamation of a Kentucky colonel without the goatee, a chain-smoking Oxford don and the American eagle on a slightly wrinkled dollar bill. Ragan's credentials are of long standing. The position and the department are new and unique. It is a commentary on Governor Robert W. Scott's and the state's interest in its heritage and creative talent that this department has been established.

"Life is lonely indeed for anyone who has never opened his mind to art, beauty and richness," said Scott, officiating at the swearing in of North Carolina's first Secretary of Art, Culture and History.

"Sam Ragan sees physical facilities as colorful storehouses . . . his work has helped preserve our heritage and North Carolina has been the better for it."

Sam Ragan, the state's first Secretary of Art, Culture and History.

Old Salem is a restoration of the early North Carolina Moravian settlement, an island of serenity in the heart of the city of Winston-Salem.

The first fire engine in North Carolina can be seen today at Old Salem. This hand-pumped engine was demonstrated for the first time on May 25, 1785. It could project a stream of water to the weather vane on top of the church at Old Salem, the highest point in the village, which was used as a fire drill target.

The new Secretary is not only a poet but a publisher-editor and has been professor, television commentator and former executive news editor of *The News and Observer*. Now editor of *The Pilot* in Southern Pines, Ragan is the author of two books of poetry as well as works on politics and journalism. He has a national reputation in journalism, having served as president of the Associated Press Managing Editors Association and as director of the American Society of Newspaper Editors. He has participated in many cultural projects and has been chairman of the North Carolina Arts Council, trustee of the School of the Arts in Winston-Salem, member of the Library Resources Commission, a past chairman of the North Carolina Writers Conference and moderator of a number of literary forums.

His column "Southern Accent" has introduced many new writers, among them Guy Owen and Reynolds Price. "If you pay attention to writers, the writers develop," says Ragan, who has done just this in his column, his creative writing workshops and his courses at North Carolina State University. Now he will be expanding those efforts, for he talks enthusiastically of how he wants to see people "both enjoy the arts and be-

come involved. A total involvement that will come about through getting more programs to the people and encouraging both local and regional art councils and historic groups in restoration.

"One of the most direct ways is carrying out programs with the state Department of Public Instruction," Ragan says. "That way you reach the school children and then touch the parents." He will be going to the farthermost corners of the state to "stir up ideas" and "find out what people want." A man with both practical and provocative ideas, he has many thoughts on how to make the state's fine art collection available to all the people, as well as ways to provide more income for professional arts people who still have a hard time earning a living.

Last year Agnes de Mille, speaking at the National Council of the Arts, said that North Carolina and New York are leaders in the arts of America. "We have taken a little money and made it go a long way," says Ragan. "The North Carolina School of the Performing Arts has attracted national attention and the North Carolina Arts Council, taking advantage of federal, state and private funds, has started countless programs to encourage creative endeavors such as literary, photographic, music, craft, dance and drama projects."

Silver-haired, courtly Sam Ragan, as one of his newspaper friends says, "is not one of the dilettanti. He's a practical fella." His deceptively soft drawl cloaks sudden flashes of wit and the observations of a compassionate, intensely human person who has a genuine feel for what the man in the street thinks and is interested in.

"If I am successful, we will see the arts touching the lives of every person in North Carolina," says the new secretary.

His enthusiastic approach is reminiscent of his poem "The Call."

> The voices kept saying
> Come on, come on.
> And the walk went through the valleys,
> Sometimes the hills.

We have the feeling that the voice of Sam Ragan will be heard throughout the valleys and the hills of North Carolina saying, "Come on, come on," to human creativity wherever it may be found.

Orton Plantation

Once, a long time ago, there was another Southland, but daily it grows more remote and faraway. Turning off the modern highway and taking the sandy, curving road to Orton Plantation near Wilmington, the twentieth century becomes the illusion and a world of moss-draped live oaks and forsaken rice fields, flooded with water, becomes reality. The rice fields have seen the stooping figures of many slaves harvesting the grain. Sinewy, well-muscled black bodies gleaming with sweat, as they labored where the wild duck and shy sunning turtles now splash.

A small chapel rises in Greek perfection, white as sun-drenched bones. Flesh and blood no longer gather within to worship, but its beauty is as timeless as the warm sunlight of a spring afternoon. The walkway from the chapel is banked with azaleas and wanders through oaks and pines festooned with moss and Cherokee roses. For a while the path seems aimless, but without warning there looms, huge and impressive, the magnificent, white-columned house for which all else is the setting. The sensation is overpowering that this house and the still ponds surrounding it are the real world, and the highway traffic and city a few miles distant cease to exist.

Surrounded by giant trees and beautiful gardens, one of the last plantation homes of the state, Orton Plantation, near Wilmington, represents the spacious grandeur and a way of life in the ante-bellum South. Because it was used as a hospital by federal troops, it was not burned as were many other fine plantations. Shown here is the chapel.

Eastern North Carolina—
An Undiscovered Song

Eastern North Carolina is a land dotted with beautiful swamps filled with mysterious, shadowy places, home of towering cypress trees mirrored in dark waters, abode of terrapins and other creatures, a place to hear the nightly chorus of katydids and bullfrogs. It is a countryside of small towns and people with time for chatting and friendliness. Across it flow the Haw River, Rocky River, Deep River and Little River, all joining the Cape Fear, life line for many an early Scottish settlement. To the south meanders the amber-colored Lumbee, winding and twisting its way like the Cape Fear through the farmland among fields of cotton, corn and tobacco until both rivers arrive at the ocean.

Traditions in the eastern part of the state follow the seasons. In the spring there are church homecomings—a yearly renewing of friendships and loyalty to the church of their "raising." In July and August come the family reunions, always occasions to anticipate, but now even more so with offspring and family increasingly scattered. On the tables under the trees, the food is almost as traditional as the reunions—fried chicken, country ham, deviled eggs, pound cake, lemon tarts—and lots of kinfolk who still claim to be "kissing cousins." Many of the old homes are still in the same family, so it is homecoming in a very real sense.

October and crisp fall days mean country church ingatherings, attended not only by members of the church but townspeople nearby. Each church takes pride in maintaining its reputation for good barbecue. On the evening before, wood is hauled in and a blazing hickory fire built in the long pit over which the meat will be roasted. All night long the men exchange stories, feed the fire and turn the pork shoulders. The meat roasts slowly, smoke curling about it, a tantalizing aroma rising and drifting out into the night air. By dawn the men will begin to cut up the meat, seasoning it with a hot sauce,

the ingredients of which are a well-guarded secret known to one of the church members who has a well-earned reputation for the making of the barbecue. Bowls of chicken salad, buckets of cole slaw and a profusion of homemade cakes are brought in by the women. Many of the cakes will be auctioned off, and it is not unusual for wealthy members of the church to contribute bales of cotton to the auction. An ingathering may attract as many as a thousand people for the noonday and evening meal and be so successful that it is the only fund-raising event for the church budget. If it is one of those warm North Carolina October or November days—days that pause like a golden persimmon almost ready to fall from the tree—there will be dinner on the grounds, and children, faces smeared with icing from sampling an unbelievable variety of cake, climbing over the cotton bales and playing while parents talk. For the early settlers, these ingatherings were not only a social occasion, they were a sharing with God of nature's bounties, for the cotton had been ginned, the meat was ready to cure and the corn was binned.

But along with these warming, pleasant customs, for some there has always been poverty amid a potential for plenty and a song yet to be sung. Mechanization moves across rural North Carolina and the small farmer struggles for a while, then leaves the land. Tenant shanties stand abandoned, left to rot or be claimed by the voracious kudzu vine, as they sag darkly in the middle of a field like sway-backed mules. There were three hundred thousand farms in 1935, almost half of them were gone by 1970, and the number continues to dwindle. Only the larger, mechanized farms survive. Cotton and tobacco are still king, and in October acre after acre of fields white with cotton line the roadsides. There was a day when driving along sandy roads you could see the pickers, both black and white, dragging heavy tow sacks behind them as they bent over the plants and moved down the long rows. Under a large oak or sycamore tree, the cotton was brought by the pickers to be weighed and piled on gunnysack sheets.

"It used to take half a dozen men to pick a bale a day," says W. T. Hancock, Scotland County farm agent. A skillful picker in prime cotton could harvest 250 to 300 pounds in a long, sweltering day. Now, gargantuan mechanical pickers lumber through the fields covering two or more rows at a time, long steel fingers picking swiftly in a manner no "John Henry" of the cotton field could ever equal. The machines pluck fifteen to twenty bales a day—a bale is about fourteen hundred pounds before it is

ginned and about five hundred pounds afterward. Instead of the trucks heading for the gin loaded with bulging gunnysack sheets and tired but smiling pickers perched on top of them—invariably wisps of cotton blew off the truck, clinging to grass and bushes like a light snowfall—the cotton is now transported in long metal rectangles similar to small freight cars. As soon as a mechanical picker is full it backs up to the metal wagon and dumps its fluffy white load as many times as necessary to fill it, then another wagon is moved up to take its place. The picker is much more efficient but not very picturesque.

The black and white field hands have moved to town or gone north, perhaps, to something better. But the money was "good" for the times and there was singing in the fields as they picked from dawn to dusk. Few white people had a cook in September and October. No matter how dependable she was the rest of the year, when she said, "It's time for me to go to the cotton," she went. Not even the offer of wages to match or surpass cotton-picking money could persuade her to change her mind. For it was the companionship of friends, the time to gossip, to sing together, to wipe honestly earned sweat off the brow, gulp deliciously cool water and sleep at night as wonderfully, physically tired as a child after a strenuous day.

Although cotton, tobacco, corn and soybeans dominate the landscape, the climate is ideally suited to a variety of truck crops, and additional income is sorely needed in

these eastern North Carolina counties. Cucumbers are grown under contract for a pickle company, but few truck crops other than tomatoes, and sometimes they have rotted in the fields. The farmer has been at the mercy of buyers who wait until the crop is so ripe he must sell at any price. Without reliable marketing facilities and nearby canning and freezing plants there will be no substantial growing of produce. Farmers will continue to grow crops that do not have a high element of risk.

Present-day farming in eastern North Carolina.

New crops mean new methods and it isn't easy to encourage farmers to learn new methods when their boys are leaving the area to look for jobs. The small farmer has always scraped along. Able to keep his independence but rarely able to buy the tremendously expensive new mechanized equipment that could make his operation really profitable. If the sons of eastern North Carolina go to college and find a job elsewhere, they seldom return. The warm nights filled with the odor of bay, pine trees and cotton dust know them no more. They have left for Detroit, New York or one of the southern cities where they endure the traffic, live on a tiny plot in a housing development or in the deadening anonymity of an apartment like the one next door and the one next door to it. Sometimes when dogwood blooms or the red mittens of the sassafras tree flame along the roadsides in fall, or a white funeral wreath appears on a door, there is a longing for the life of the small North Carolina towns left behind where there was time to see and time to care. But always the question "What work is there to go back to?" must be answered. And the answer is usually the same.

Cotton has always been woven into the fabric of North Carolina life, and the mill villages with their monotonous rows of tiny white houses are still a familiar sight. Although most of the houses are no longer owned by the mill and have been sold to the workers and the "company store" is a thing of the past. The textile industry has been an important source of employment in North Carolina, but for the most part it is a low-paying industry and men and women who are unskilled labor or semiskilled may often be discarded as easily as they are hired. Mechanization has taken the place of people for rooms in the mills which were once filled with workers now contain long rows of machines that have taken over the tasks of human hands.

Most encouraging are the new, small industries local leadership has attracted and sold on the advantages of an ample labor supply, a mild climate and the advantages of small-town living. New technical schools are making an important contribution training local people for these industries and providing the type of job instruction which will play an important part in attracting more new industries to eastern North Carolina, filling the skilled labor void that has existed in the past.

Between the coastal plains and the Piedmont is a land of sandy hills and warm winters, a land that is not quite the red clay of the Piedmont nor the flat, sandy plains of the coast.

Occasionally snow comes to the cotton fields of North Carolina. The last of the cotton was picked a month before. Now, a field once white with cotton is white with snow.

The sandhills are the home of Pinehurst and Southern Pines, a place of golf courses and riding trails, of tree-shaded streets and ever-increasing resort development. James W. Tufts of Somerville, Massachusetts, one of the early carbonated-drink magnates, used part of his fortune to establish the town of Pinehurst where golf and thoroughbred horses soon became part of the accepted way of life. In this same "land between" north of Pinehurst near Seagrove were people who used their hands to make pottery instead of putting. As settlers emigrated into the Piedmont and mountain sections, the abundance of clay in the area around Seagrove, Asheboro and Sanford started a string of potter's wheels turning as did the abundance of streams turn gristmills.

The earthenware was covered with glazes made from minerals also found nearby. Once there had been a great mountain range called the Uhwarrie Mountains and the massive upheaval of earth and rock that created these mountains millions of years ago brought to the surface a score of minerals—iron, galena, copper, gold. As the mountains wore down long before the white man came, they left for the early settlers a supermarket of minerals, and the potters were able to make glazes that would come out of their kilns in hues of green, blue, brown, white and orange. In addition to the minerals and the clay, the land yielded pine knots and hardwood to fire the kilns. For six, seven, eight generations the potter's wheel has turned in this "land between" the plains and the mountains, first supplying pottery for the settlers moving west and now becoming a mecca for those who appreciate the vessels from skilled hands and the potter's wheel.

Fortunately, progress skipped over parts of this land and on Carolina byways the potters continue their heritage. Recently a Potter's Museum has been opened at Seagrove and an effort is being made to preserve one of the unique folk arts of the state. Names like Owen, Cole, Teague, and places like Seagrove and Jugtown in the sandhills remind one of the words of Jeremiah, "Then I went down to the potter's house and behold, he wrought a work on the wheel." The traditional forms are now joined by contemporary shapes wrought by new craftsmen attracted to the area, and thus, the old traditions are side by side with highly individual modern designs. Instead of molding the people as the rocky highlands of Appalachia creased furrows on the faces of the settlers, this land was made to be molded by those who took the clay in their hands and shaped it into objects of usefulness and beauty.

The Golden Weed

Tobacco is to North Carolina what oranges are to Florida or wheat to Kansas. The history of the state, its early settlement, as well as the present economy are tied in numerous ways to what the farmers called "the golden weed." As tobacco farming changes, so does the landscape of the state alter in subtle ways, for tobacco is grown in nearly all of the one hundred counties—flue-cured tobacco in the lowlands and burly tobacco in the mountainous regions.

Every Tarheel school child knows the story of Sir Walter Raleigh's servant who thought his master was on fire when he first saw him "fuming" and dashed a pitcher of water on him to save his life. Perhaps he has also seen the engraving by James Egan depicting the knight smoking as he reclines languorously with a pipe that looks fully six feet long. The pipe is decorated with feathers and on his writing table stands an open round box of tobacco. The "Virginia" leaf was grown from seeds taken back to England after an abortive attempt to colonize Roanoke Island or the mainland then called Virginia. Colonists were disappointed not to find gold (the motive behind many an early exploration), but the golden leaf they took back to England with them also turned out to be valuable.

All over the low country, the tall green tobacco plants grow in fields of four or five acres—there are few tobacco barons in the state. Almost yearly, allotments dwindle, forcing marginal farmers off the land. In January and February the long tobacco beds covered with white cloth look from a distance like rectangular sheets of ice. After the weeding comes the transplanting by tractor and machinery, a loud click telling the two riders ("setters") when to drop the six-inch seedling while water is simultaneously released.

By early summer tourists on their way from Florida to the Carolina mountains can see the green stalks growing tall as a man's shoulder, leaves broad and rumply with thick veins branching out beneath white, noxious blossoms that have to be topped.

Tobacco barns dot the landscape of eastern North Carolina. Often they are placed near large shade trees so the workers can find relief from the summer sun.

66

Late July is the time to gather in the tobacco leaves and tie them to sticks which will then be hung inside the tobacco barn until heat changes the green leaves to gold.

Clare Leighton, the English artist, has commented on the beauty of the tobacco barns, comparing them to the deep-eaved farm buildings of the Austrian Tyrol. Her woodcuts have caught their dignity. In a sense, they symbolize eastern North Carolina with its straight lines that spurn embellishments, its sloping, open sheds and squat doors, front and back. The roof is often tin, streaked with orange rust, the barns themselves weathering a soft gray. Looking at their silhouette you understand the kind of honesty and beauty that James Agee discovered in the tenant shanties of Depression Mississippi.

The old hand-fired brick furnaces are gone now and so are the old curing methods. The farmer does not have to sit up all night tending the furnace as if he were cooking cane syrup. He sleeps in his bed rather than out at the tobacco barn, coming out only occasionally to check the thermometer of the automatic gas or oil-fired curer and adjust the thermostat. The automatic curer has taken much of the guesswork and skill out of fixing the color in the bright leaf. And the folkways of the farmer have changed, too. Some of them may look back to the old yarn-swapping sessions and chicken stews held around the tobacco barn at night, but few would wish the night's long labor back.

Mechanization explains the out migration of Negroes and whites. There are few mules left or black sharecroppers working the green, flat fields. Instead of hands there are tractors and mechanical harvesters that need fewer workers. Women and children who once tied the tobacco on long sticks in the shade of the overhanging eaves of the tobacco barns are often replaced by a huge sewing machine that sews the heavy green leaves on the sticks.

Already the prosaically constructed but efficient new bulk barns with forced heat are appearing, and by the end of the '70s the revolution in curing techniques will have covered the entire state. Brick furnaces and log or frame barns will be relics of the past.

On the campus of Duke University there is an imposing statue of tobacco tycoon James B. Duke and somewhere a statue should be raised to a young black slave named Stephen because he invented the new method of curing that revolutionized the tobacco industry after 1839. The story goes that one night Stephen fell asleep when he was firing his master's barn. In those days the fires burned in the open on the dirt floor. When he awoke the fire had nearly gone out. As Stephen piled on the wood he forced the heat up, just at the right time, and the tobacco turned a rich golden yellow never obtained before.

The year's work of this farmer is being evaluated by the keen eyes of the buyers. The auctioneer's chant will tell the farmer whether he has made a profit or not. This same scene takes place each year in the late summer and early fall on the floor of tobacco markets (called warehouses locally) throughout eastern North Carolina.

When his master, Captain Abisha Slade, took the six hundred pounds of special gold leaf to the Danville, Virginia, market, it brought four times the average price. The "Slade method" of curing with charcoal and raising the heat after the leaves were partially cured spread beyond the captain's home in Caswell County, and thereafter North Carolina became the "bright leaf" center.

During August and September eastern North Carolina highways are crowded with farmers bringing their golden weed to the tobacco markets—the big trucks haul it in huge hogsheads to the drying plants and Piedmont factories. Warehouses have changed little in the last decades. Stifling hot, long, low buildings with skylights let in the Carolina sunshine and everywhere there is the strong aroma of the cured tobacco. An auctioneer lifts his singsong chant as the tired and sweaty buyers follow him on either side of the bright rows, going through the ritual of stooping to examine the quality of the leaves.

As each tobacco belt opens, the rhythm of life changes. Small dreamy towns suddenly awaken to a frenzy of excitement, merchants are full of anticipation, streets are clotted with farmers and trucks on their way to the warehouses. When the last of the tobacco is sold and the buyers move on to another belt the towns settle back to sleep once more.

It was shortly after the Civil War and purely by chance that Durham became the center of tobacco manufacturing. During the last days of the war, soldiers in both blue and gray collected at the village of Durham's Station, where John Ruffin Green owned a small tobacco factory catering mostly to students at the University of North Carolina at Chapel Hill. Soldiers on both sides took to "sampling" his wares—in effect, taking away a liberal supply. Green was cleaned out, but at least the Yankee soldiers did not burn his building or destroy his equipment. After the war was over, the mustered-out soldiers recalled the fine aromatic flavor of Green's smoking tobacco. From every corner of the country they began writing to Durham, until the orders flooded the little factory. This led to the world-wide fame of Bull Durham tobacco and the beginning of North Carolina's domination of the tobacco industry along with the tenant farmer, sharecropper culture which persisted for many years until mechanization replaced it.

North Carolina's
Woman Country Doctor

"It was almost midnight when I got a call to go to Worley Pace's home," recalls gray-green-eyed Dr. "Jo" Newell. "We were having one of the worst ice storms I'd ever seen, but from his wife's description of his symptoms I knew he'd had a coronary. Worley lived about nine miles from here and a swamp with a bridge over it led directly to his house.

"I started out in my brand-new Buick. There were chains on the tires but as I approached the bridge I could feel the car begin to slide, turning as it slid along. It finally came to rest against the bridge abutment, completely blocking the road. I got out and, holding on to the car, walked around to see exactly what had happened. The ground was like glass beneath me and I found myself slipping off into the frozen swamp. Every time I tried to crawl up the bank I'd slide back.

"In the distance I saw a light from the Richard Thompson house (diagonally from my position, across three fields) and decided to try to get there and phone for an ambulance for my patient. It was impossible to walk. Every step or so I found myself falling and on one of the falls I broke my right arm. I kept on until I managed to reach a cornfield, then I lay down on my stomach and, reaching out my left hand, I grasped cornstalks and pulled myself along. That's the way I finally got across the field and up to the house.

"Much to my dismay there was no one at home. I broke a window and got in. Although there had been a power failure and the lights were not working, the phone was and I called Wilson Memorial Hospital for an ambulance. When we finally arrived at Mr. Pace's it was necessary to slide him on a stretcher two hundred feet to the ambulance. As we tried to raise the stretcher, we kept dropping it. My patient's arm had been ankylosed by arthritis, but when he became apprehensive and I asked him to hold

Country doctor Josephine Newell conceived the idea for this museum, unique in the United States (Bailey, North Carolina).

The doctor's office has a doctor's roll-top desk and an early telephone. A third room in the museum contains exhibits of early medical instruments, saddlebags, microscopes and memorabilia.

my hand, he reached for it with the arm he had not been able to move! Perhaps because he had been jarred so when they dropped the stretcher."

Five feet four and every inch reflecting boundless energy, Dr. "Jo," as her patients in Bailey affectionately call her, begins talking about why there are not more doctors in rural practice. In eastern North Carolina there is one doctor for every seventeen hundred persons.

"I think medical schools are aiming young doctors in the direction of the cities. Then, too, they are near larger schools, a country club and their families can have more social life."

At East Carolina University in Greenville, North Carolina, Dr. Edwin W. Monroe who is vice president for Health Affairs says, "I am sure you can find reasons which depict many different viewpoints. . . . I feel quite simply that North Carolina faces this problem for the same reason that most other states face it: namely, the apathy and lack of concern within the state by the institutions and people responsible for the production of health manpower."

Dr. Jo Newell thoroughly enjoys rural practice, saying, "I've been here twenty-one years and loved every day of it. I like the people. We're like members of a family, and I take time to talk to my patients."

Shortly after World War II, Josephine Newell's fiancé died, and her father urged her to abandon chemical engineering, in which she already had her degree, and become a doctor—perhaps because there had been six generations of doctors in the family! At twenty-five she went to Bailey "for a year's experience in general practice in the country." Postmaster Jack Collie bet her fifty dollars that she wouldn't stay the year out, telling her, "There's too much work, it's too hard and the county roads are mostly sand and dirt." On January 1, 1952, she collected the bet and Collie, filled with admiration, sent her two dozen roses as well. He has continued to send the roses each January 1, even though he is now an invalid.

"My practice runs the usual gamut of diseases, but I don't do any obstetrics," says Dr. Newell. "There was so much to do, I couldn't do it all. After a year, I dropped obstetrics and now I refer those patients to Wilson. As a matter of fact, I need a partner and I've been trying to find one. It's very hard to get a young man or woman to come to the country and I've had no luck thus far." Bailey is a small town with a population of two thousand. Although Dr. Jo obviously enjoys her work, she would welcome sharing her practice, for she is seldom through at the office before eight o'clock and then must go on to see patients in the Wilson Hospital. Coming home for supper about ten, she takes a break before making her round of house calls which last until midnight or later.

"We visit the old people and try to help them adjust and we work toward helping the families adjust. The old people are happier if they can be at home, and the families are, too, because they don't feel guilt ridden."

"There are people here who have been an inspiration to me," reminisced Dr. Jo, "for instance, Mr. Lafayette Boykin, 'Mr. Fate,' as everyone called him. He never had any sickness. He chewed tobacco, dipped snuff, smoked a pipe, cigars and cigarettes every day of his life, and never had heart disease or emphysema. He was sick one month and died of acute leukemia at ninety-two. When he was eighty-five, he was still an avid fisherman. Wearing hip boots, he would trudge out to Contentnea Creek every day to fish. One day he came home dripping wet and his wife asked him what had happened. Mr. Fate had slipped on a rock and had to swim out of the creek in his heavy hip boots."

Dr. Newell owns the modern building that houses her clinic where she has her own laboratory and does much of her own lab work, although some is sent to Wilson. Many of her patient referrals are also sent to specialists there. She received her medical degree at the University of Maryland, later interning in Woman's Hospital in Baltimore and Rex Hospital in Raleigh. Her colleagues not only have a high regard for her ability, but a feeling of affection that parallels that of her patients.

"I love my life and I wouldn't swap it for anyone else's," says Josephine Newell. The people of Bailey wouldn't swap Dr. Jo either, for they have admonished her, looked after her for several weeks when she had an auto accident, carrying her from a wheel chair into her office daily, and for many years depended upon her concern.

In a technological society we often try to solve our problems using technological methods, and exciting breakthroughs continue to occur. But the ultimate answers to people problems lie with people resources—compassionate, intelligent human beings like Dr. Jo who will share their own time listening and responding to the needs of their fellow man.

Passing of the General Store

No one ever dashed into an old-fashioned general store to make a purchase. The leisurely pace of both clerks and customers would have made such a thing unthinkable. My own grandfather found time to manage a large store called MacRae Company in Maxton, supervise three farms, serve as Mayor and occupy a cane chair tilted back against the storefront on warm spring days.

Inside, the store was cool and more than a little dark with its dim, ball-type lamp fixtures. Shelves extended along each side wall stretching upward from floor to ceiling, and in front of the shelves with just enough space for the clerk to walk were the long oak counters with glass fronts. I recall taking pair after pair of black patent Mary Janes home with me joyfully, my grandfather never protesting. My delight in choosing innumerable pairs of shoes was never dimmed despite the fact that the next day they had disappeared and were back on the shelf in the store.

A large glass jar filled with sugar cookies and sacks of green peanuts to munch were another attraction, as was the huge round of sharp cheese that sat on the back counter. On the floor in front of the counter were barrels of dried field peas, salt mullet, molasses and shiny tin containers of seed. With great plans for my own garden in the back yard, I would choose a few seeds from each can, dropping them all into my small brown paper sack. For a city child like myself there was the never-ending fascination of hand pumps, kerosene lamps, horseshoes, bins of assorted nails or bamboo fishing poles, which were stacked near the open front doors on the first spring day so they could be seen from the street. Most of the stock ran to farm supplies, horse collars, bridles, plows, axes, "Saturday night special" metal bathtubs, overalls, snuff and other dry goods such as underwear, shirts and fabrics, except at Christmas time when the bicycles magically appeared.

On the long, hot summer days the store was a cool retreat from the heat of the day and the pavement that scorched bare feet. A place to explore among the boxes, eat

cookies and wheedle until about four o'clock when my sixty-eight-year-old grandfather who still enjoyed swimming (and tennis) would finally turn the store over to his clerk and take me to the creek. Barney, his collie dog, rode on the running board of the car and went swimming with us.

But, as I grew older, new dresses became very important and the small selection of utilitarian fabrics at my grandfather's store no longer interested me. I transferred some of my affection to "Mr. Ed's" (Carrowon & Company) a block down the street. This was the store for the gentleman farmer and his family. Many of the brands were just like those in the big city store. Many a summer afternoon was spent trying to decide on dress material, choosing patterns and selecting trim. From Mr. Ed's came the pink piqué for the frock with the scalloped hem and the red and white check for my first really daring dress with its see-through layer of organdy around the midriff.

Except for the greater selection of merchandise, the store looked much like my grandfather's—high ceilings, dark wood floors and black iron coal stove in the center of the floor. Carrowon's along with MacRae Company struggled through the Depression while many stores around them closed their doors. In later years businesses came and went on the town's Main Street, but Mr. Ed's stayed. It became something of an institution. Young girls shopped there as their mothers had done before them. Seen through the eyes of youth, it was not even a remote possibility that Mr. Ed would grow old or one day be unable to operate the store. He had always been there and always would.

Some said he still had shoes, hats and dresses left from his stock when the store had first opened. He didn't believe in sales and had a real aversion to cutting a price. But he gave good service and sold a dollar's worth of merchandise for a dollar. He was a friend to his customers, giving credit without interest when it was needed, and he always had a joke to relate. Mr. Ed was more than a businessman. He was a volunteer fireman as well, who rarely missed a fire as a volunteer or later as Chief of the Fire Department.

After forty years Mr. Ed had his first real sale and his last. It was his "Going Out of Business" sale. At first no one could believe the splashy big letters on the windows. On the opening day before the doors were unlocked there was a large crowd on the sidewalk waiting in line. The sale lasted for a week and then the merchandise was gone—pointed shoes with buttons, dresses from the twenties, even the old J. P. Stevens thread case.

Mr. Ed laughs at one of his own jokes.

The next morning Mr. Ed sat by the coal stove as he had done for over four decades, gazing at the empty store and bare shelves, then got up and went out the front door, locking it behind him as he had done so many times. He didn't pause to look at the sign that said "Once in a Lifetime Sale," but walked the two blocks to his home. That afternoon he sat in the swing on the porch of the big white frame house. There were not to be many years of sitting on the front porch swing watching the cars go by or the children walking home from school for Mr. Ed's health was poor. Before long the swing and the street that had known his tall, bony figure for so many years knew him no more.

Although one general store after another is passing from the North Carolina scene, there are still a few of the old family stores left. And new country stores like the one at Burnsville and Southern Pines have appeared, perhaps, because there will always be a fascination for most of us in browsing around a store that is not a specialty shop but seems to stock everything from apple corers to rock candy, slates, dough boards and dinner bells.

The Dreaming Miller

In a time when solitude did not have to be sought but was a way of life, when a man's own fields were a hewed-out clearing fringed with misty green woods, the early settler would set out in a wagon bearing his grain to the miller. An important man this miller, who could take the grain, give back the flour and in so doing yield the bread of life. Map makers of colonial days knew the location of every mill, and such a one was Dillon's Mill. It ran continually to supply the demands of both settlers and Indians.

Said to be the oldest mill still operating in the state, it is located a few miles north of the jet airport which serves the Greensboro, Highpoint, Winston-Salem tri-city area. Coming in for the approach to the airport, many a passenger has flown over the mill, whose giant water wheel turns as it did in the days of stagecoaches. Legends abound about old mills and this one is known for the story of the dreaming miller. Historian John T. Brittain of Asheboro tells it this way: "James Dillon was the miller in Revolutionary days. On the night of the 10th of February 1781, he had a strange dream. He dreamed he had his toe burnt. Dillon and his wife were among the many Quakers who had settled in the colony. His wife said to him, 'James, Thee had better not go down to the mill this morning.'

"But on going to his door, Dillon looked out to his mill and saw the British soldiers grinding and feeding in full possession. He hurried down, thinking to control the situation. Almost at once the soldiers began firing on him. Dillon ran and hid behind a tree. One foot, however, remained exposed. A soldier fired—and the shot struck Dillon in the same toe which he had dreamed was burnt."

Down through the years, while other mills crumbled from disuse, Hedricks Mill (which the mill was now named) with its millhouse of stone and great hewn timbers saw a steady succession of millers. The last of these may be the present miller, Lloyd Lucas, who has been a miller for over forty years, as was his father before him. Shoring up the old timbers and modernizing the equipment, Lucas continues to use the centuries-old millstones, turning out water-ground wheat and buckwheat flour, cornmeal and grits for the community. A tall gaunt widower, Lucas raises some of his own grain, although much is still brought to him by nearby farmers. He does not know who will follow him someday or whether someone will, for a technological society has little patience with the pace of a mill or with dreaming millers.

Another famous old mill is Winebarger's Mill in the mountains near Boone. Walter Winebarger's craggy face is untanned, the pale hue of a man who has spent his life indoors. His overalls are coated with a white powder and so is the interior of the huge mill including a few cobwebs among the rafters. Winebarger has been a miller since boyhood, as were his father, grandfather and great-grandfather.

Down upon the noisy grinding stones beneath the mill he pours his daily oblation to life, the ancient offering of grain—corn, buckwheat or rye. The building vibrates with a rhythmic clatter of the large bolt that sifts the bran from the flour.

The Winebarger Mill was built by the present owner's great-grandfather. "He would give one day of his labor as a carpenter for two days' help working to build the race for this mill." The mill race is a long one—the water comes rushing noisily down Meat Camp Creek almost half a mile to power the huge wheel. The millstones originally came from France and are called French "burrs." Bags of grain are stacked everywhere, even up the sides of the walls, for Winebarger receives a tremendous number of orders for his water-ground meal. It not only tastes differently, the texture and quality are scarcely similar to meal produced by the large electrically powered mills and sent to the shelves of most chain stores.

A free man in the most modern sense of the word, the old-time miller was not restricted by feudalism nor was it necessary for him to belong to a guild. He had no competition in his area, for bread was an essential part of diet and he could grind the farmer's grain in his own good time.

When Winebarger starts his machinery it is nothing like an electrically powered mill, and after pollution prohibits the use of some other forms of power, perhaps we will return to water power. When the machinery starts, the entire building seems to surge and vibrate as the huge wheel with its paddles begins to turn. You feel the hand-hewn beams shudder and you must shout to be heard. You become part of this power. It surrounds you, exciting the senses, and you know why a man loves being a miller and will be a miller as long as he lives.

The third generation of the Winebarger family now operates the mill.

The Hamlet Station—
Storehouse of Memories

There is a railroad station in a place called Hamlet which was once one of the principal stations on the Seaboard Airline Railroad between the northern cities and the deep South. It was a big station for a hamlet, but for the thousands of people who remember the heyday of the Silver Meteor, the Silver Crescent and the streamlined trains which used to glide in and out on the glistening rails, the Hamlet Railroad Station was the border crossing between the cold winds of the snowbound northern winters and the palm trees of Florida.

New Orleans and Atlanta trains switched off here and followed the east-west tracks so that the station sat in a triangle of railroad tracks. The New Orleans- or Atlanta-bound train would curve around on the long sweep of the triangle so that it was impossible to reach the station without crossing tracks in every direction. Now there are just two passenger trains left, one going southward at 8:50 at night and the other coming north, stopping at Hamlet at 4:20 in the morning.

The turret of the station stands like a guardhouse on some imaginary line over-looking the yard, and to further enhance its status, the Hamlet stop was as long as the one at Philadelphia, Richmond or any of the other major cities. The stop was longer, primarily, because Hamlet was a division point on the railway and often the crews were changed here. Its location also meant that many of the sleek passenger trains that ran during this busy era of passenger service would arrive near midnight.

At night the station with its floodlighted tracks was the center of life for the town. Hamlet people would walk over there to talk and watch the trains come and go. Restless passengers would get off, stretch their legs and stream into the newsstand or cafe across the street to take advantage of the chance to buy untaxed cigarettes. The sales of cigarettes in Hamlet over the years, if ever discovered by a researcher in the next cen-

tury, may cause long and ponderous thoughts in the scientific community as to why the people in this area were particularly resistant to lung cancer, for the per capita purchase was probably fifteen packs per day! But, of course, most of these packs were tucked away into suitcases and coat pockets as the trains came and went in what appeared to be a never-ending stream of silver cars.

During World War II trains were crowded, passengers often sat on suitcases, crowded into washrooms and even between cars. The station swarmed with men in uniform. The east-west line, which ran from Wilmington to Charlotte and beyond, crossed the north-south tracks just outside the big, curved waiting room with its hard wooden benches. Soldiers on pass from Fort Bragg, eighteen-year-old draftees heading south to Columbia, officers on leave pacing up and down restlessly mingled with civilians waiting for trains filled to capacity and watching the large blackboard on which arrival and departure times were chalked in. The stopover was a welcome one for passengers since the trains were not air conditioned and fully as much soot as cool air often came in the open windows.

The passenger depot, built in 1900, was one of the first manifestations of the Seaboard Airline Railroad, formed through a merger of more than a hundred smaller lines. It was the epitome of the twentieth-century railroad station, opening the first year of the new century. Yet, today, it appears as if it has always been there and few people in Hamlet can ever believe it was not.

Recently, the building was added to the National Historic Register and justly so, for the image of this building and the station has certainly been engraved in the minds of thousands of people. The Seaboard Coastline plans to replace the terminal with a "compact, modern facility." There is a modernistic little AMTRAK sign dangling incongruously from the overhanging roof of the old station that, hopefully, can be taken down and put on the next ghost train to Washington. And the new railroad management would do well to put their "compact, modern facility" somewhere up the track a bit and let the local people of Hamlet keep their station as a museum—at least that is what it will officially be called.

It is really a unique storehouse of memories, that should be a memorial to all who have stood and waited, voiced greetings and good-byes, watched and loved trains in a day when trains were trains and a station had a personality all its own.

Where Have All the Tom Sawyers Gone?

This Tom Sawyer and Huck Finn story was photographed in the early days of the sixth decade of this century. The sixties have ended and with them, perhaps, the opportunity to do many other stories like this one. Time is running out for haunted houses, millponds, turtles and old barns.

Entertainment is purchased at a store, prepackaged right from the factory in the Pliofilm wrapping, very antiseptic.

So here are the pictures of maybe the last Tom Sawyer we shall see. And where have all the Huck Finns and Tom Sawyers gone? . . .

No more secret places for children to go and get away from adults. No more paddling through the cypress trees on the millpond of a hot summer afternoon. (The pond is being drained for a factory site.) No parks and recreation departments have yet planned and received authorization from the county commission to build a haunted house. Nothing was planned for the boy during the summer these pictures were taken. It was just a disorganized summer of fun and exploring which made learning a happy, exciting adventure.

Are the orange day lilies still out there? Is the Queen Anne's lace still white among the tall weeds? Somewhere, we know they must be, along with the odor of the wet, old dark wood and the wonderful chance of finding something exciting.

The Piedmont—
Growth, Concrete and Culture

The British came back. Lord Cornwallis who left his name on the road leading to this building would be surprised to find that a British drug company, Burroughs Wellcome, built this futuristic complex for its research laboratory and American corporate headquarters. The Research Triangle Park, conceived by former Governor Luther Hodges, is now a reality with more than two dozen major companies and government agencies occupying research and laboratory facilities. The points of the Triangle are UNC at Chapel Hill, Duke Univeristy at Durham and North Carolina State University in Raleigh.

Early every Monday morning in Charlotte where three hundred of the top five hundred companies in the nation have branch offices, salesmen and manufacturers' representatives are telling their wives good-bye and leaving their suburban homes, apartments, condominiums and townhouses, which fringe the city, to begin five days of sales calls and meetings that may take them to many cities and many states. Some will drive and some will fly, but most of these men will be out of town all week returning on Friday night. For many of these families, Charlotte is a temporary home—a place to live for perhaps three years until their company transfers them to another city. There is a natural reluctance to put down roots, to become too deeply involved in the churches, schools, civic or political life.

An understanding of the problems and needs of a city the size of Charlotte requires an investment of time a tired businessman with only his weekends for relaxation does not have, nor do wives who must act as head of the family during their husbands' absence. For a number of these people, Charlotte is just one of several places where they have already lived or will stay briefly during their corporate career.

So, the affairs of the city are for the most part left to a dwindling number of native Charlotteans. Many of the people subject to frequent transfers do not know the background or voting record of local candidates when they go to the polls. Some do not register to vote while they are here, and their knowledge of state government is even more limited than what is happening at city level. Yet, this county of Mecklenburg has the largest voter registration of any county in North Carolina, due to its high population density, and could be a vitally important influence on the direction of state government. The vote cast in some Charlotte precincts may be as large as that of an entire county in other areas of the state.

Sometimes it is disheartening that so much electoral power is in the hands of so many people who, through no fault of their own, will never have time to grasp what is happening in Charlotte or in North Carolina or to climb the political and civic ladder to positions of influence which would allow them to contribute their abilities and fresh approaches.

While leaders in the tri-city area of Winston-Salem, Greensboro and High Point are beginning to discuss how to combat urban sprawl and to consider green buffer areas and satellite towns to control growth and make life more pleasant for the citizens they already have, the word in Charlotte still seems to be GROW. And, as we grow, so do crime, traffic, pollution and an ever-increasing burden on our municipal services.

One Charlottean says, "My neighbors down the street moved here because Atlanta was getting too big for them. We'll soon remedy that!" North Carolina's "Metrolina"—the ten-county area of which Charlotte and Mecklenburg County are a part—has over two hundred people per square mile and is outranked in the South in density only by Atlanta, Miami, Tampa and St. Petersburg. So, if we begin to suffer a few more dented fenders at the shopping center, get the jitters about driving in traffic, wait in line at ticket offices or supermarkets, it's all part of playing the numbers game and trying to catch up with Atlanta.

The Chatham County Courthouse with its red brick and white columns sits squarely in the intersection of U. S. Highways 15, 501 and 64. In the late afternoon, it looms as a three-story milepost for the traveler on the highway. Landmark or milepost, it is still a courthouse in Pittsboro, a small town one county south of the booming Chapel Hill and the Research Triangle area.

The Fourth of July parade at Faith, North Carolina, stretches from one end of the town to the other. There are floats, pretty girls, marching bands—all the things a parade should have. And yet, in the middle of the parade between antique cars and tanks from Fort Bragg, marches a Confederate color guard looking as if it had not heard of Appomattox. With the passage of time memories have dimmed, but there is still a charisma about the image of Confederate soldiers and silence and respect as they pass.

A passing motorist might think this wagon train was an apparition out of the past. Yet, horses and wagons have not passed entirely from the Carolina scene. Now, several wagon trains make annual trips in various parts of the state, reliving for a few days the life of their frontier forefathers.

If Charlotte heeds the statistics in the new *Metrolina Atlas*, takes its air pollution problem seriously, and begins to solve its urban problems, it will be one of the most desirable and stimulating cities in which to live. Cultural opportunities abound at Ovens Auditorium, the Coliseum, the Mint Museum, the Charlotte Nature Museum, the Symphony Orchestra, the Opera Association, the Oratorio Singers, Little Theatre and twenty-one colleges in the Metrolina area. A few miles away, Gastonia has a Music Education Foundation unique in the United States, and the Schiele Museum of Natural History has been recognized throughout the Southeast. Lake Wylie and the Duke Power State Park on Lake Norman contribute to this exciting atmosphere of outdoor recreation, intellectual stimuli and the arts. Newest asset to the Piedmont is Carowinds, an amusement area near Lake Wylie which approaches the scope of Disneyland, providing "magic kingdom" type rides and amusements and emphasizing the history and culture of the Carolinas. The days of the Catawba Indians have been re-created, a magnificent southern plantation lives again. The cities of Old Charleston and Old Wilmington are here to explore, as they were a century ago.

At dusk a panoramic view of the city of Charlotte may be seen from the rooftop of a building off Independence Boulevard. The sky reddens as the sun sinks lower. Smoke rises here and there along the northwest rim of the downtown skyline. At the right of Covenant Presbyterian Church steeple, off in the distance looms King's Mountain, high and long across the horizon like some mighty fortress of old. The center city is a cluster of skyscrapers, their walls honeycombed with lighted office windows. These are the business firms and financial institutions of our state which deal not only in commodities and sales outputs but in decisions affecting the lives of many North Carolinians. Across the city skyline stretches a snakelike stream of smoke from the stacks of a nearby plant, gradually turning the glowing sunset into a murky backdrop for the clean lines of the towering new buildings. The skyscrapers are in the palm of a huge hand with streets like fingers stretching out from it into the suburbs, where trees become so thick their tops form a lush canopy over invisible homes and apartments, inhabited by invisible people—loving, hating, hoping, sharing the life of this largest of all North Carolina cities.

The lights of Charlotte appear almost simultaneously—turned on by hands electronic as well as human. Now, the view has changed to that of a flattened, illuminated

There is a shopping center now, where cattle once grazed. The buildings of downtown Charlotte are seen in the distance.

Christmas tree. The taillights of autos become red streaks as if the lifeblood of Charlotte was flowing along the streets. At 7:10 a jet streaks northward over the city, its passengers looking down at the flickering multicolored lights spread out like a kaleidoscope beneath them. The lights below extend for miles, and one is more than ever aware of how the edges of many North Carolina cities reach outward daily, devouring the land, skyrocketing property values until to farm this countryside longer would be ridiculous—a fist of flesh flung into the concrete face of progress with predictable results.

But not all of the Piedmont is talking as if it shares Charlotte's ambitions. "Charlotte has already said it wants to be a big city, another Atlanta. While Greensboro and High Point have almost grown together, there is still time to preserve an illusion of open space," says Lindsay Cox of Greensboro, executive director of the Winston-Salem, Greensboro, High Point Council of Governments. Just as the areas between Charlotte and the small towns around it are growing together, increased urban and commercial development among these three cities will eventually cause "a sprawling megalopolis without a focal point like Los Angeles. Greensboro Chamber of Commerce Vice President William Little believes that a good medium-size city is better than a big bad one. Other ideas under discussion are encouraging single family houses with yards (not as profitable for the builder who wants to get the most people into the least space), continuing to keep golf courses and recreation areas within fifteen or twenty minutes' ride from homes and, who knows?, someone may even revive the idea of sidewalks! When influential business and community leaders become interested in "people needs" there is no telling where they will lead.

Where there once was a highway through green country between Greensboro and High Point, roadsides are lined with pizza parlors, furniture and carpet stores, trailer sales lots, and only Bragg Boulevard in Fayetteville can compete for ugliness. Where there are still miles of farm land and open land left, lower tax rates will be proposed to keep them that way. It has been done elsewhere in the country; it should be done in North Carolina. There must always be roads to take on a Sunday-afternoon drive through the green, rolling hills of the Piedmont, near our cities and accessible to all. If we do not decide now on those things we would like to preserve for tomorrow, they will slip away from us unnoticed.

Ten thousand or more Canada geese migrate each fall to winter at the Gaddy Wild Life Refuge near Ansonville. Visitors come from miles around to see them. The refuge was established through the efforts of Mr. and Mrs. Lockhart Gaddy.

America's First Gold Rush
Happened Here!

The history of the North Carolina gold rush is written in clay—red clay where after a rain a Cherokee Indian might have found a gold nugget in the sunlight. But now the nuggets are gone and with each rain a little of the history, a little of the red clay filters down farther, filling the old shafts and pits of America's first gold fields.

Still scattered across the Piedmont are wooded areas where the ground has the appearance of an old battlefield pitted with holes and scarred with trenches. No armies fought here, only thousands of Welsh, Cornish, Austrian, Polish, German, Italian, French and other immigrants side by side with Carolina farmers armed with picks, shovels and gold pans, each fighting his personal battle with the hard, milky-white quartz and red clay. There were gold diggings from Cherokee County east to the Piedmont and in the Piedmont from the Virginia line down into South Carolina. Gold was discovered in over sixty North Carolina counties, with many of the best-known mines in the Charlotte area.

By all rights the seventeen-pound gold nugget, a veritable boulder of gold compared to the pebble that started the California rush, should have been discovered by Hernando de Soto. But the Indians gave Hernando the runaround. He went marching off to greener fields and over a century later, in 1799, it was a twelve-year-old boy, Conrad Reed, who found the golden rock. No isolated find, it lay gleaming in the sunlight of a shallow stream bed filled with hundreds of other nuggets—a stream that would later be described by author Thomas Jefferson Hurley as "the richest mining claim in America" for gold nuggets—richer than any single claim in California.

The idea of finding gold was so absurd in the sleepy little village of Concord, North Carolina, that the silversmith there looked at the rock and proclaimed it worthless, for obviously it was not silver. However, since it was extremely heavy, it made an

A gold panner at Little Meadow Creek, where a seventeen-pound gold nugget was found in 1799. From this stream came hundreds of golden nuggets. The initial discovery here started the Carolina gold rush and the location is both a state and national historic site.

excellent doorstop for the Reed farmhouse, and it was almost three years before Conrad's father, John Reed, decided to take it with him on a trip to Fayetteville. He had always been curious about the rock and now he wanted a jeweler to look at it. The jeweler recognized it as being almost pure gold. Reed sold it to him for $3.50. Later, he discovered that he had been swindled out of several thousand dollars, but the jeweler reimbursed him for part of the sum.

More important, however, is that when John Reed went back to Cabarrus County, he found there were many gold nuggets on his land. A report by the director of the United States Mint to President Jefferson in 1805 confirms that the first native gold arrived from Cabarrus County and that the gold fields there were reported to be "rich and extensive." Boom towns with stores and taverns sprang up overnight. At some mines the prospectors were so eager to reach the gold that they didn't even take time to throw up a shack, but simply stretched blankets across poles for shelter, and these crude tents clustered near the mines. Hucksters congregated around the camps, their wagons laden with provisions to sell to the men.

Thus began the years when North Carolina earned its reputation as the Golden State, thousands of miners continuing to arrive from a score of European countries. From 1804 to 1828 all the domestic gold coined at the Philadelphia Mint came from the North Carolina gold fields. Charlotte became a thriving gold mining community, and on December 4, 1837, a branch of the U. S. Mint opened at the corner of Mint and Trade streets, ending the profitable business of waylaying shipments of gold on their way to Philadelphia. Within the present city limits were many mines—the St. Catherine, the Barringer and the Rudisil. Names of the Mecklenburg County mines were as colorful as the gold they yielded, for there were the Black Cat, the Queen of Sheba and King Solomon's mines. Merchants left their stores, ministers abandoned their pulpits, and as one traveler put it, "You could hardly get across this county without falling into a gold mine!"

Even now, no one can talk for long about the Carolina gold rush before mentioning Gold Hill, a wild and boisterous boom town with all the glamor and legendary characters of any town in the West. After the first discovery of gold there in 1842, the next fourteen years saw these mines yield millions of dollars' worth of the precious metal. In 1848 Gold Hill had at least fifteen active mines, employing a thousand or

Dogwood blooms where men once dug for gold, The old diggings at the Howie Mine in Union County are gradually being covered by vines and underbrush.

more men, along with five stores, four doctors and one tavern, says Wheeler's history of North Carolina. If John Wheeler was right, the most profitable business in Gold Hill may have been the single tavern, for a newspaper account after the Civil War reports twenty-seven saloons!

Gold coins, both privately and officially minted, began to come into circulation in a land where cash of any kind was scarce. But at country stores and taverns throughout the Carolinas, gold dust was the poor man's currency, and many a farmer and miner picked out his supplies while the store owner used his scales to measure pennyweights of gold dust in payment. For a young nation with no Fort Knox gold behind its currency, the Carolina gold rush saved the eagle and the dollar from being dependent upon foreign sources of gold.

Remnants of the old superstructures and mine buildings may still be seen around the town of Gold Hill and just outside Waxhaw. The most famous mine of all was the Reed—America's first operational gold mine as well as the site of the first discovery of gold. The Reed has been purchased by the state as the location of a museum and restoration so that it may forever remind the people of North Carolina that America's first gold rush began here.

Molasses Making
in the Southern Highlands

Long before city dwellers' thoughts turn to pumpkins and Indian corn, it is time for the first ritual of fall in the North Carolina mountains. When crisp days arrive with dogwood and sumac ablaze throughout the woods and along the roadsides, farm folk begin molasses making.

It is really a kind of sorghum sorcery, for the green wands of cane are magically transmuted into delicious, fragrant amber syrup. "You can't let the cane get frost hurt," warns one farmer, "or the molasses won't be any good." Each family grows its own cane and has its favorite varieties such as Honey Drip, Foxtail, John-the-Baptist or Old Timey Red. Since frost comes early to the mountains, molasses making begins by mid-September. This is a pioneer ritual—a custom handed down from the earliest settlers for many generations—an event to savor and anticipate.

It is a brisk September morning as Eckard Murray picks his way along the steep, rocky road leading into his valley with its field of sorghum cane. Mist still rises from the stream beside the road. Sunlight sweeps across mountain ridges burnishing them red and gold, warming the slightly stooped shoulders of the old man. Expertly his strong hands lay hold of the cane, cutting the tall red-streaked green stalks with their spikes of reddish seed at the top and placing them in an ever-growing pile. Wood smoke begins to curl skyward above the crude mud and fieldstone furnace used to heat the juice for many an autumn past.

"Rocks hold the heat in better," says Murray. He has placed a long metal tray on top of the furnace for the cane juice. Not far away stands his horse tied to a twenty-foot sourwood sweep or beam, which is attached to the center axle of the cane mill. A "lead" pole is used to keep the horse plodding patiently in a circle while Eckard Murray, with his small granddaughter watching, feeds eight-foot-long stalks through the

Stripping the sorghum cane before making molasses.

"Mule power" crushes cane.

Skimming the green foam off the molasses.

mill's gears to extract the juice. Some of the stalks never reach the mill but are popped into young, eager mouths that know the delight of chewing freshly cut cane.

The sweet, pale green liquid runs into a keg and at intervals is poured from the keg into the tray where it bubbles and burbles, giving off a fine fragrant aroma as it thickens. This is an occasion for neighbors to gather. Grownups and children make the long walk into the valley to help and to enjoy the simple pleasures of swapping stories and tasting the cooking syrup. Men and women with the lines of living etched strongly on their faces lean against the side of the shed near the fire. They trade news of good fortune and bad, of children now grown and gone to work in the city. Not much talk of national politics, not much complaining—just occasional good-humored jibes and a bit of teasing. Threading the conversation is a concern for each other, along with an acceptance of life and hardship.

The hill folk are not clock watchers nor do they try to time the syrup very carefully. The pace of their cooking, like the rest of their living, proceeds at a slow tempo—a more ready willingness to wait than is found in the outside world. Some of the farmers use a tractor, but others like Eckard Murray still use mule power for their cane mill. At intervals someone rises and stirs the juice, skimming off the green foam that rises to the top of the bumptiously boiling liquid, or thrusts more logs into the flames evoking a shower of sparks. Making molasses is an all-day task.

Children ignore warnings not to get too close and come up to peer impatiently into the steaming pan. By midafternoon the first of the liquid is ready to taste and thick enough to pour into the waiting jars.

The sun slides lower behind the tall purple mountain at the head of Eckard Murray's valley, and with jars of molasses under their arms, his friends begin the walk back down the mountainside. Often called "long sweetenin'," it will be trickled on hot biscuits or slathered on cornbread during the winter months ahead. A widower now, Eckard Murray shares his syrup with his daughters and their families. The last to leave, the old man in his faded blue overalls walks alone to his cabin, carrying a few jars of the "long sweetenin'" to pleasure himself until the sorghum cane grows green and tall and ripe for cutting again. A time which will say once more—this is the end of summer, the beginning of fall. In ways like this the months and years of the mountain people are marked off on the calendar of life.

Their Name Is on Our Waters

A Cherokee brave gazing into one of his tribe's sacred quartz crystals a century and a half ago would never have recognized his people's land today. Only the black, rippling waters of the Oconaluftee River flowing swiftly along in the sunlight were there then, receiving Cherokee warriors morning and night as they cleansed themselves for four days following a battle, listening to the chant of the hunters reciting sacred formulas as they bathed in the water before hunting, rushing unwary trout toward the fish traps and giving water for the large gourds the Indian women dipped into the stream and carried back to their small log houses.

In the season of the first New Moon of Spring and later the Green Corn festivals and October New Moon Festival, the rhythmic, pulsating sounds of the drums and the chorus of singers' voices dancing the religious dances would float out over the river, sometimes mingling with the mist. During these week-long celebrations, the men would try to foretell the events of the coming year. A brave who stared into the sacred cyrstal and saw himself lying down would ask the tribe's priest to look. If he then appeared to be standing erect, he was ordered to bathe the mystic number of seven times in the river—assurance that he was safe from death for another year. Many a night in the moonlight, the tall figures of Indian braves could be seen as they plunged into the black waters of the Oconaluftee.

Ceremonial uses of the river long ago faded into the dimness of the Cherokees' unwritten past, but today, near its banks are campgrounds, motels and stores with names that echo an earlier era—the Big Arrow Campground, the Chief Motel, the Owl Trailer Park, Little Beaver Craft Shop, One Feather Trading Post and the Qualla Gift Shop. Here at the Qualla Reservation, the Qualla Arts and Crafts is a unique cooperative enterprise, owned and operated by the Cherokees to perpetuate the highest quality art and craftwork of the Indian people. It is an important source of income for 208 members and their families. Here one may find the traditional double-woven bas-

Sunlight streams through the center opening into the seven-sided council house at Oconaluftee Indian Village restoration in Cherokee.

TSALI
CHEROKEE BRAVE, SUR-
RENDERED TO GEN'L
SCOTT TO BE SHOT
NEAR HERE, 1838, THAT
REMNANT OF TRIBE MIGHT
REMAIN IN N.C.

kets of river cane or hemp, original wood carvings, pottery, beadwork and books of Cherokee legends and folklore.

Not far from the river are the Cherokee High School, a modern garage, a feed and seed store and a building supply center. Instead of Indian braves bathing in the moonlight, many of them are taking part in one of North Carolina's most popular historic outdoor dramas—*Unto These Hills*. The summer nights are filled with music rising from the large mountainside amphitheatre. In a magnificent natural setting with the Smoky Mountains for a backdrop, present-day Indians, descendants of the Cherokees who lived the story, play important roles in a tragic but sometimes triumphant narrative. It begins with the arrival of De Soto in 1540, builds to a climax with the cruel removal of all but a remnant of the Cherokees dragged from their homes and, under the command of General Winfield Scott, sent on the long and painful journey westward to Oklahoma. Four thousand men, women and children died along the way. There is the dramatic battle of Horseshoe Bend where Chief Junaluska not only helped President Andrew Jackson defeat the Creek warriors but saved Jackson's life when he was at the mercy of a Creek tomahawk. There is the moving episode of the heroic Tsali who gave his own life so that a handful of his people might remain here in the land of their forefathers. Tribal dances highlight the story, among them the magnificent Eagle Dance. Nearly three million people have seen this living lesson in history, which begins the last week of June and continues until early September.

Along with ancient rituals and tribal customs, the language, too, has been dying out, and now the Cherokee tongue is being taught to the Indian children in their school. Of this last Indian tribe remaining in North Carolina an early writer said, "Their name is on your waters—ye may not wash it out."

Perhaps if a brave of two hundred years ago came back to walk the banks of the Oconaluftee, he might meet a small Indian girl or boy playing beside the water and be able to learn in his own tongue something of what has happened to his people, although it would not be possible for him to talk with many of the older Cherokees who have largely forgotten their native language. But a bright little girl or boy would suggest to the brave that he go to the "village," for the Oconaluftee Indian Village, established in 1952, depicts the life of two hundred years ago with astonishing accuracy. Here our Indian traveling through time from another century would find the same mud and log cabins of his own day and the same skills employed. Women are using the mortar and pestle to grind the corn meal for bread which was eaten with the wild game. Others weave baskets using Cherokee designs handed down from mother to daughter. Ropes of clay are being molded into pots, arrowheads shaped for warfare, and a young man is making locust darts with fluffy thistle tails to be used in hunting small animals. Now and then he rises and tests his darts in a bamboo blowgun. Each dart strikes near the bull's-eye of his target. Smoke rises from logs being burned out for dugout canoes. The canoes were the property of the tribe rather than an individual.

In times of war, a war chief called Kalanu and his organization replaced the peace government much as a military government or martial law has sometimes replaced civil government in the white man's civilization during times of crisis. The war chief wore red and the peace chief wore white.

The Cherokees were a religious people believing in a creator god called Yowa (surprisingly close in pronunciation to the Hebrew name Yahweh) whom they considered to be a unity of three beings. They also believed in the existence of spirits and the afterlife. A priest was singled out in childhood for special religious training. Today, all vestiges of the old religion have vanished, due in great measure to the zeal of early Baptist missionaries, although there are churches of several denominations on the 56,000-acre reservation.

Nearly five thousand people of Cherokee ancestry are numbered in this Eastern Band of Cherokee Indians living on the Qualla Indian Reservation and governing themselves. It is hard to realize that 56,000 acres are all that remain of the territory of a once powerful and proud tribe—territory that encompassed large portions of what is now Virginia, Tennessee, North Carolina, South Carolina, Georgia and Alabama. The Cherokees are holding fast to their heritage, preserving it in their language, drama, museum, village, crafts and rich legendry.

Stories handed down from one generation to another still linger, and one of the more fascinating is the story of the magic lake. Westward from the headwaters of the Oconaluftee River where it rises in the wild depths of the Great Smoky Mountains, there is an enchanted lake called Ataga'hi. Hunters who have strayed into this wilderness area tell of hearing sounds like the whirring of thousands of wings as if a tremendous flock of ducks has been startled and is rising into the air nearby. Cocking their guns in excitement, they press through the underbrush and come out at the edge of a great open flat of land without birds or animals or even a blade of grass.

This is the enchanted lake. And because no water can be seen there, some think it dried up many years ago. Not so, say those who have sharpened their spiritual vision by an all-night vigil of prayer and fasting. When the first rays of the morning sun appear, they behold the purple waters of a magnificent lake with springs spouting from the cliffs around it. Its waters are filled with all sorts of swimming and flying creatures. Fish leap joyously upon its surface, ducks from overhead skim over it leaving a silvery wake. Around the shoreline animals of all sorts are gathering. It is the medicine lake of the birds and animals and to this water all who are wounded may come. An animal making his way through the woods and plunging into the water emerges on the other side with his wounds healed. It is, of course, necessary for the animals to keep this lake with its enchanted water invisible to men.

Perhaps the secret of its healing source lies in the rippling waters of the Oconaluftee. Someday its murmur as it winds through Cherokee may speak the secret that will heal the wounds early white settlers dealt their brothers—the First Americans. Mankind has for too long known the ways of hurting without learning the ways of healing.

The Other World of John West

Shifting masses of clouds shrouded the ridge of mountains with tall, faraway peaks suddenly visible through the fog, only to disappear and minutes later reappear in mystic, eerie fashion. The gray sky yielded a steady drizzle of rain.

It was the day Appalachian novelist and poet John Foster West had chosen for us to accompany him as he revisited his childhood home in the red clay hills of Wilkes County.

We left Boone, riding with John Foster, a tall, lean mountain man who maneuvers his green Volkswagen with a kind of restrained ferocity, gathering all the speed the car's tiny motor has, zooming furiously past other vehicles on the downgrade and muttering under his breath if a car pokes along ahead when there is a pass lane. Watching John's intent Romanesque profile it was easy to visualize his father standing behind a tree near his house, rifle pointed, ready to take care of any "devilment" from a trifling neighbor.

Have you ever felt that you have visited a place before, seen the houses, known the people? As John Foster West, the Sixth, drove into his boyhood world, there was the feeling of having been there before, for it was just as he had described it in his novel *Time Was*. The countryside, the houses, the old store building took on an uncanny familiarity.

"That is where 'Doc' Ellis lived, and over there was Cousin Bill's house. We're passing the store in the book," said John and then he pointed to the hilltop where the home of the hated Hill Anderson had once stood.

The roads, once dirt, are now paved, but they are still the old wagon roads twisting around the sides of the mountains, following meandering stream beds as they have done since the first frontiersmen settled these hills. Turning down a red clay ribbon of a road that undulated over the hills for several miles, the Volkswagen finally slowed and stopped. On the left was a field of wet, orange broomstraw and set back from the road crouched a sagging cabin, its boards blackened and weathered.

John Foster walked the overgrown scraggly path to the cabin and stood on its rotted porch. We quietly followed him through the kitchen door, not wanting to interrupt his thoughts or anything out of the past that might still be happening there.

"My mother and father's bed was here. In the corner of this room I was conceived and born. Over there against the wall was a bed and there were three big beds in the other room for the seven of us children." The windows of the little three-room cabin had been broken out long ago and vines twisted and curled about their empty frames. Through one of them could be seen the grotesque branches of the old pear tree.

"This little stone fireplace was all we had for heat. My father's sister burned to death standing in front of a fireplace like this one when her long dress caught fire. It happened to many a woman. They had a habit of backing up to the open fire. Poor people didn't always have underclothes to wear in those days, either. I can remember my mother and sister doing that, standing close to the fire and pulling up their dresses to warm their backsides. My father carefully laid these stones for the fireplace and chimney in home-made clay mortar. Every bit of this house he built with his own hands—the floors, walls, shingles—all of it.

" 'Here is where I'm going to put a center hall someday,' Dad would say, looking at this long room across the back." But there were many mouths to feed and many rows of corn to hoe and no time left for center halls for John West, the Fifth. Only an occasional moment to stand under the shade of the pear tree in summer and wipe sweat off his furrowed, leathery skin as he looked out over his rows of corn—or a chaw of tobacco to turn with his tongue by the fireside in the winter months.

Nature has taken the farm land back now. Bull's Branch still runs past the old pasture grown up in forest where tulip, poplar and pine vie for room—Bull's Branch, which the hog killer in *Time Was* used to say Daniel Boone's trail once followed.

On a lonely hill in Wilkes County, souvenir hunters have chipped away at the headstone over Tom Dula's grave. Made famous by The Ballad of Tom Dula, *the truth is that Tom Dula received a fair trial and was defended by North Carolina's most famous lawyer at the time, former Governor Zebulon Vance, a Civil War hero.*

John West recalled a few lines from a poem he had written about that.

> "If at this moment he should come along,
> Striding up the branch in coonskin cap,
> I would meet him on familiar ground.
> He would need to know what happened here
> Between his day and mine. "Not much,"
> I'd say. "Six generations come and gone,
> A good many crops of corn, no spring now."
> The comfortable green forest all around
> Would put him at his ease, and he could choose
> to disbelieve that time had passed at all;
> For even time stumbles and stays its pace
> Passing among tall trees."

"For years Dad hauled tan bark and lumber at three dollars a load to North Wilkesboro to pay for this land—dirt that wouldn't sprout a pea but for two hundred years grew shaggy corn.

"Not far from here was the blacksmith shop where two men worked. I remember Dad telling about the day they got in a fight. One had a hatchet and the other a knife. The man with the hatchet hit the other fellow cutting off the top of his head at the same moment the other man opened his stomach with the knife. 'Doc' Ellis sewed up both men and they lived to a ripe old age.

"This morning in my writing class at Appalachian University we talked about when we first knew what death meant and that we were mortal. I had gone with my parents to a house where two old ladies had died. All the grown people were sitting around talking in low hushed voices. I didn't know what it was about and I got tired of staying in the room with them. So, slipping out, I went into the back hall where I saw two sawhorses with boards across them and a sheet over the top. I tried to climb up to see what it was and lost my balance. As I fell I clutched at the sheet and pulled it down with me. When I got up and looked I was terrified. There were the two old ladies stretched out. A few days later our family milk cow was struck by lightning and killed.

My older sister and I found her that morning and my sister started crying for she knew how much the milk meant to our family. That night my first realization of death came when I looked at my empty milk glass."

Many people know John Foster West for his book *The Ballad of Tom Dula*. He had heard the story as a child from his mother and father, and his grandfather was a member of a party that searched for Laura Foster's grave. " 'Tom Dooley' was one of the earliest songs I sang and the murder area was just a few hills and hollows away."

These memories of his early life are all part of the character of this earthy, compassionate and talented man, who now lives in a mountain chalet near Blowing Rock. As he teaches students poetry and creative writing, he continues his own work (two books are at the publishers) and is working on a fourth novel called *The Long Way Home*. He is a writer who knows how to communicate about life and people, and like the description in the folk song about John Henry—John Foster West is a "natural man."

Folkways of the Coves and Hollers

There is many a fascinating character back in the coves and "hollers," but some are very suspicious of strangers and others are neither loquacious nor able to analyze the complexities of the mountain folk. That is why a man like Cratis Williams is such a rare find.

Dr. Williams, professor of English and dean of the Graduate School at Appalachian State University at Boone, is a native of Appalachia, educated at the University of Kentucky and New York University, who speaks of the mountain culture with both objectivity and experience. It is fortunate for Appalachia that he returned, for this man with the humorous twinkle in his eyes and the neatly trimmed beard is probably without peer as an expert on the folklore of the southern mountains.

Widely sought after as a speaker and conductor of folklore workshops, Williams is not only author of *Ballads and Songs of Eastern Kentucky* and numerous other articles, but he is an inexhaustible source of information on mountain speech, a fascinating teller of tales in the mountain idiom and a gifted ballad singer.

"The mountaineer is not homogeneous racially and culturally as he is often presumed to be," says Williams. "Just as he himself is a much more complex person than is generally supposed, so his speech is more difficult to describe accurately. When written down, contemporary mountain talk brings back memories to Midwesterners of ancient grandfathers and lusty companions swapping yarns around pot-bellied stoves in crossroads stores.

"Even the most illiterate mountain folk are familiar with the contents of the King James Version of the Bible, frequently through oral tradition, and biblical quotations find their way easily into mountain speech."

Although almost embarrassingly candid in their comments about each other, Dr. Williams says, "Mountain folk are scrupulously punctilious in observing manners and exchanging civilities. Imbued with the principles of equality for which their great-

A tree loom is used by Phyllis Yacopino, an instructor at North Carolina's craft school at Penland. A wide variety of craft skills are taught and practiced here. Businessmen, doctors, lawyers, housewives come to Penland to learn such diverse skills as pottery making, hand weaving, glass blowing and metal work.

The "Parson of the Hills" walks toward a mountain cabin followed by Santa Claus and children. It is Christmas Day and the Parson is bringing Christmas to some of the remote homes of the North Carolina mountains. Actually, the Parson of the Hills is the Reverend Charles Keyes of Hickory who has worked in the western North Carolina area all his life to reach mountain families not served by any church.

Billy Graham drew almost one hundred thousand persons to hear him preach at Grandfather Mountain during the annual "Singing on the Mountain." The event is a traditional occasion for gospel singing and evangelism.

grandpappies 'fit' at King's Mountain, they consider themselves as good as anyone and often a heap better than 'them lowdown onery neighbors up the creek a ways.' Generous and eager to be helpful, they expect in turn favors, not words, for thanks. Mountain people speak to one another when they meet and a stranger tramping through the mountains soon learns to speak to people if he 'values his hide.' "

"There is just a little quality of violence about us, too," says Dr. Williams with his gentle smile. "Mountain men are fond of fights. If someone is 'stobbed,' the affair is referred to as a knifin'; if shot but not killed, a shootin'; if killed, a killin'. After the fact, a killin' may be referred to as a little killin', and the murderer often chooses to refer to his predicament modestly as 'that thar little trouble I am in.' "

The middle-aged mountain man is likely to be harsh in his evaluation of youth. If his daughter slips away to peep at a young swain "on a tear," the father is almost certain to be merciless in personal references to the budding suitor.

Edd Presnell, "King of the mountain dulcimer makers." Banner Elk near Tennessee line.

"Reckon the leatherheaded eedient hain't nuver thought a breath o' haow plumb dangerse it is to run his hoss a-past folkses' haouses, a-hollerin' and a-shootin' off his old pistol thataway. . . . W'y, if his brains was dannymite he wouldn't have nough to blow his hat offen the top of his head. A body'd hope he'd be as willin' to work as he is to lope the roads. . . . His pap, afore he was penitentured daown in Georgy, didn't hardly nuver work none to speak of. Go aout a day now and then and fight them brars and burshes on that little old rabbit ranch o'hisn like the devil a-beatin' tanbark fer a little whaal and then git so disheartened from a-goin' araoun' and araoun' like a 'lasses mill and a-not a-knowin' wharabouts he was at that he'd take and go off to the woods some'eres and make hisself a little run o' who-shot-John."

Mountain men are fond of displaying their strength and are greatly admired. Often their feats are exaggerated and memorialized in the folk tradition. The man of unusual courage is likewise praised. "If his ire is aroused, his own prickly rhetoric mounts to superb heights of Elizabethan prose and he announces that he is 'half hoss and half alligator and can stomp down and chaw up blood raw, bones and ha'r and all, ary that ever drapped from his mammy's womb.' The wrathful mountaineer's oaths, sworn in rolling rhythms and punctuated by blue notes of fury, are often fractured with magnificently compounded parentheses of scurrility, abuse and low obscenity."

Among uncorrupted mountain folk honesty is highly esteemed, especially the repaying of debts. It is a matter of pride to "owe naught to no man" at the time of one's death.

The thrifty mountain family is disdainful of loafers and spongers. "If them sickenin' buzzards was my boys, they'd not laze around me and eat me out'n house and home. I'd kick ther haunches higher than ther heads, so hard they couldn't set down fer a week, and put 'em in the cornfield.

"And ever' Satidy night—and Sunday, too, a heap o' times—people a-pilin' in on ther old man from all o' hell and half o' Georgy a-eatin' his grub and a-feedin' ther beastes his corn while ther pore old mammy, already wore down thinner'n a whupperwill, packs and fetches fur 'em. Ther pore old pap a-mukin' down, mealy mouthed, and a-takin' it. . . . He jest sets back and don't say nary word o' no kind to them thar sapsuckers. Jest snailmozies around as slow as 'lasses in Jinewary. Fust thang he knows he'll wake up some o' these hyar mornin's and find hisself finaciously ruent."

Pioneer homestead at entrance to Great Smoky Mountains National Park.

The mountain way of life has always lent itself to the epic tradition, and among the old folks, stories are still told of strange and fabulous characters whose exploits have grown with time.

In his article, "Fabulous Characters in the Southern Mountains," Dr. Cratis Williams says, "Strange women were also reported from time to time. James Lane Allen, the Kentucky novelist, toured the mountains of southeastern Kentucky. The most famous hunter he became acquainted with was an Amazonian woman who had trained her dogs to go into the woods for game while she sat in her cabin door. At the time Mr. Allen met her she was old and infirm, but in her youth she had been able to whip strong men in single-handed combat. Even in her old age he said of her, "A fiercer woman I never looked on.""

Charles Dudley Warner, traveling in western North Carolina in the early 1880s, spent a night in the home of Big Tom Wilson, the hunter and guide who had found the body of the famous botanist Dr. Elisha Mitchell. That night Big Tom entertained his guests with hunting tales and stories of his exploits in the mountains. Warner was puzzled, for there was something hauntingly familiar about his host who told the stories simply and expertly without seeming to brag about himself. Finally, Warner realized that Big Tom was a replica of Leatherstocking in Cooper's novels.

These people, strangely like the heroes, ogres and witches of word-of-mouth stories current in the area, have not only added zest to the life of many a mountain cove and valley but they have been models for some of the most colorful characters that have appeared in the fictional interpretations of mountain folk, says Cratis Williams, such as Jesse Stuart's *Taps for Private Tussie*, Henry Giles's *Harbin's Ridge*, Harriette Simpson Arnow's *Hunter's Horn* and *The Dollmaker*.

Mountain folk singer "Doc" Watson.

Thomas Wolfe and "Altamont"

"In the haunting eternity of these mountains, rimmed in their enormous cup" lies "Altamont," identified on maps as Asheville. But it is really two cities, that of Tom Wolfe, who on the pages of his books preserved it in time as it was in the early years of the twentieth century, and the Asheville of today. It would have pleased Wolfe that he had just once defeated his lifelong antagonist, time—"And time passing . . . passing like a leaf . . . time passing, fading like a flower . . . time passing like a river flowing . . . time passing . . . and remembered suddenly, like the forgotten hoof and wheel . . ."

The bricks of the old sidewalk in front of 48 Spruce Street turn their wet, worn faces upward to the visitor. A fine rain falls and dusk comes darkling about the eaves of a rambling old Victorian home. It is easy to imagine that nearby is the spirit of a man who never really left. For this most famous address in Asheville is now a shrine to Tom Wolfe. It became the Altamont of his great novel *Look Homeward, Angel* and his bitter descriptions of a place in which he felt himself imprisoned caused him to be an outcast for many years. But later the work of their young literary genius became a source of pride to Asheville, and the Pack Memorial Library now has an extensive collection of his books and memorabilia.

His boyhood home, once the boarding house Tom Wolfe named "Dixieland," would now present a satisfying, freshly painted exterior to his mother, the strongminded Julia Wolfe who cooked on the great wood stove and industriously canned fruit and vegetables for her boarders' table. Every possible room was turned into a bedroom for boarders until finally her own family was crowded into small, cell-like rooms and even forced to eat in the pantry.

There is an impressive glimpse of the mature Tom Wolfe in the bedroom that has become a repository for the furnishings of his New York studio. There is a surprising likeness to the room of Carl Sandburg's, just a few short miles away at Connemara. Neither writer made any real attempt to collect matching furniture or objects of art.

All is utilitarian. All serves a central purpose—to write. Like Sandburg's, the bed of Tom Wolfe has no headboard, and the room is crowded with books. A plain work table was sufficient for his two typewriters, and next to it stands a huge green wastebasket that must once have been filled to overflowing with discarded ledger sheets. On these typewriters he wrote *Of Time and the River, You Can't Go Home Again* and *The Web and the Rock.*

Altamont today is surprisingly similar to the city Tom Wolfe knew so well. It is not hard to gradually absorb his feeling of being hemmed in by the mountains, and he might have been grateful for the fresh wind that will enter the plateau of hills and hollows when the narrow tunnel through Beaucatcher Mountain is blasted away for a six-lane highway. The skyline is dominated by buildings of an earlier era—many from his own time. The streets that wind up and down over the hills are lined with Victorian houses. Wolfe would still feel at home in Pack Square. The Buncombe County Court House looks as if someone failed to stop the builders who kept going up, up with the foundation until finally they placed the columned top high in the air rather than upon the ground.

*Fresh flowers placed by Tom's brother
Fred mark the final home of Thomas
Wolfe in Riverside Cemetery, at
Asheville.*

The country market he frequented on Lexington Avenue is still a pleasant place to visit. During the early morning hours farmers' trucks, filled with fresh vegetables arrive, and mountain women place their colorful produce on long wooden tables—ripe red plums, smooth purple eggplant, jars of golden sourwood honey, sweet corn, red-skinned sweet potatoes, squash, fresh eggs, country butter and varieties of long, scarlet-tinged beans such as one never sees in a city supermarket. The market is no longer open at night as it was in the days when Tom Wolfe would loiter there, talking with the mountain men and women behind their tables of produce, but it lingers on as a picturesque part of this city's daily life.

The people who remember Tom Wolfe have dwindled. Asheville attorney Bill Styles saw Wolfe often as the author walked from the cabin he had rented at Oteen. "He walked in any kind of weather, and he strode along, a hulking giant of a man." His "hunger to devour the earth" made him so alive that it is hard not to see him yet, walking along with his bounding stride, staring at the old storefronts that still line Lexington Avenue.

Altamont is changing. It began as the last frontier, a vestige of civilization before travelers struck out across the mountains into uncharted wilderness, and in 1795 an unenthusiastic land speculator described it as a "town but two days' walk from the Cherokee Nation. They keep a near Sixty men out about 7 miles distant from town in small garrisons to prevent Indians from coming in on them . . ." By 1866 Asheville was established as an all-year resort for pleasure and health seekers and tourists. Less than ten years later Frances Tiernan, who wrote under the pen name of Christian Reid, traveled by stagecoach to Mount Mitchell and Mount Pisgah near Asheville. As she watched the sunrise, she exclaimed, "Dear God, I thank thee for this Thy gift, the Land of the Sky." The name became accepted as descriptive of this beautiful mountain area.

The Angel made famous in Look Homeward, Angel *is not in the Riverside Cemetery at Asheville but is located some miles away.*

Begun in 1890 and finished five years later, George W. Vanderbilt constructed the famous Biltmore House, a veritable castle on a twelve-thousand-acre estate, which is now open to the public. Vanderbilt brought to North Carolina the leading architects, artisans, decorators, engineers and foresters of the day. He also assembled the only complete collection of American azaleas. An offshoot of his interest in plants was the first forestry school in America and Pisgah National Forest—eighty thousand acres of beautiful mountain land which he and Mrs. Vanderbilt transferred to the government. Vanderbilt regarded the forest as a living organism and wanted to co-operate with the government to preserve it for the future.

Asheville is also the home of the Southern Highlands Handicraft Guild which encourages skills of the past and helps mountain craftsmen market their crafts. Some of the most exquisitely wrought work of the mountain people is on sale in the Guild Shop —corn shuck dolls, wooden carvings, dulcimers, chairs of walnut and cherry, hand-woven stoles, creative glass, enamelware and distinctive pottery. It was to western North Carolina that Josiah Wedgwood looked in the eighteenth century when he imported a fine clay from the Cherokee Indians.

One of the city's places of great natural beauty is the University of North Carolina Botanical Gardens, and most unique is the area dedicated to a Garden for the Blind. The idea came from a similar garden in Austria where there are plants the blind can touch, smell and even taste. In the Garden for the Blind are mountain wildflowers painstakingly gathered and replanted by members of Asheville garden clubs—varieties of mint, each with a different odor, joe-pye weed with its plumes of fuzzy purplish blossoms, deer grass, the fragrant spikes of clethra, sweet fern, honeysuckle and many rare native plants. The garden surrounds a fountain of brass disks that chime faintly as the wind reverberates through them. In the spring visitors may hold the sweet shrub bloom in their hand and breathe in its fragrance. In midsummer the pungent odor of various kinds of mint leaves brings delight.

Even before the highway through Beaucatcher Mountain is widened, a fresh wind seems to blow through this city. It is in the views of O. L. Shelton, vice president of the Chamber of Commerce, when he says, "There come times in our individual lives when we must make a decision as to which way we really want to go. . . . The big cities have continued to get bigger, in a feverish competition of unrestrained growth. Quan-

The Biltmore House at Asheville, often called the finest castle in America.

tity, not quality, became their god, and it was at the altar of numbers that they worshiped. But many of those who had knelt at the altar of growth are having second thoughts about the demands. For our American dream to survive, it seems clear that it will be the Ashevilles of the land which will have to find solutions to their problems while they are still of bite-size proportion, capable of solution. We can build a humane city where the individual is paramount. We can see to it that all of our people have decent homes and a suitable living environment. . . .

"If I were given the choice here of a million-square-foot building or a million new azalea plants, a million new rose bushes, a million more dogwood trees, highways and streets clean and free of a million pounds of junked automobiles and trash—then I would quickly choose all the other alternatives over the concrete and steel of a building. Because this is my town, my home where I will spend the rest of my days. I want to be proud of it and I want it to be pleasing to the eye and to the mind of the beholder. There is a new warm breeze blowing our way: It is one which should provide the self-renewal we need, individually and collectively, the determination to translate worthy goals into solid reality."

Hopefully, the "new warm breeze" will blow away the gargoyles that still haunt Altamont, and a city that even the young rebel Tom Wolfe might have liked will emerge.

"Altamont" as Asheville a half century later.

149

"This Is the Place"

High on a hill overlooking purple mountains and 245 acres of rolling fields and woods stands an imposing white-columned home surrounded by huge trees and fifteen-foot-high boxwoods.

"The first time Carl came here," said Paula Sandburg, "he put his hand on that porch bannister, looked off at the Blue Ridge Mountains, and said the same thing the Mormons said when they found what they were looking for—'This is the place.'" Oddly enough, the final home chosen by this man who had spent so many years writing about Lincoln was built by Christopher Menninger, secretary of the Confederate Treasury under Jefferson Davis.

Twenty-two years later, on July 29, 1967, after writing his final collection of lyrics, Carl Sandburg "slowly breathed away," leaving the home and the land he had come to love. The estate, which a previous owner named Connemara after the Irish district, was purchased in 1968 from Mrs. Sandburg by the National Park Service, to become an American shrine.

The house and grounds were not yet open to the public in 1972, but the Park Service hopes to open them as soon as possible. Congress has appropriated up to $900,000 for restoration although only enough money has been released to the National Park Service to begin repairs and employ a small maintenance staff. Gordon Gay, the ranger in charge, is hopeful that more funds will gradually be released. He has steeped himself in Sandburg's life and legend and is knowledgeable about both his poetry and his prose. Of particular importance is the protection of Sandburg's papers, correspondence and library from humidity damage. Some of this material is now at the University of Illinois, but thousands of books and papers remain throughout the house to suggest the presence of the man, the tremendous range of his mind and his unbridled curiosity.

At Flat Rock the poet kept to himself, guarding his privacy and making little effort

The stairs to Sandburg's second-floor office are reflected in the famous Steichen photograph in the hall of the Carl Sandburg home at Flat Rock, giving substance to the feeling of Sandburg's presence.

to know his neighbors. It was time to relax now on the wide front porch with Ralph McGill or that other famous adopted Tar Heel, Harry Golden, who would write a book about him. A time for swapping tales and playing the guitar and singing ballads. Or to stuff his pockets with sandwiches and slip off in the woods to be alone and test his loneliness. Looking over the ranging hills, on clear days as far as the Blue Ridge, Sandburg must have felt the rightness of his coming.

He had come to a state he would have liked had he been young enough to know it and grow into it. A people used to hard work, with expectations of getting ahead, who distrust plutocrats and wealth as he did, who distrust artiness and show as he did in his rugged poetry. This shaggy white-maned man who had been a poor bootblack, a potter and hobo would have found it easy to talk to the native Tar Heel. And he would have picked up many a folksong to play on his guitar and many a folk saying such as those he recorded in *The People, Yes.* He identified with the hopes and suffering of the common people: "I glory in this world of men and women, torn with troubles, yet living on to love and laugh through it all."

Although he sought no recognition, the state did not let his presence go unnoticed. The university gave him an honorary degree; in 1958 the governor proclaimed a "Sandburg Day" and made him "Honorary Ambassador of North Carolina."

Today, Connemara is much like it was on July 22, 1967, when Sandburg died. On every table and beside every chair lie periodicals.

Floor-to-ceiling bookcases cover the walls of the house—in the living room, music room, downstairs study, upstairs hall, bedrooms and even the dining room. They constitute a library of over eleven thousand volumes. A prodigious reader with the "restlessness of the seeker, the questioner, the explorer of far horizons," Sandburg's interests were as diverse as those of any man of our time. He categorized his books for convenience. There are shelves devoted to birds, animal husbandry, agriculture, insects, genetics, biology and every phase of life and the universe—photography, wood carving, theatre, archaeology, history, psychology and myriad other subjects, including many editions of his own books on Lincoln. The length and breadth of this man's inner life are here, to be absorbed from the carefully indexed file cabinets, periodicals, books and photographs. His typewriter sits with dust-covered keys, surrounded by shelves stuffed with clippings and correspondence. Conveniently close is a dime-store glass ash tray, a half-burnt cigar still resting on the edge.

Near the office is his own small bedroom, Spartan in appearance, its furniture mismated but functional. A threadbare oriental rug covering the floor is in contrast to the rough-looking bed he hewed out with his own hands. It has no headboard, just a wall of books within easy reach. On the table beside the bed is the harmonica on which he played many of his own folk songs, several of his pipes and two cigar boxes. At the time of his death he had smoked all of his favorite Webster cigars save five, which are still enclosed in their cellophane wrappers. A beer can had become a holder for sharpened pencils.

It was in this room that he kept his enormous collection of records, which he listened to late into the night. Album after album of classical music—Mahler, Shostakovich, Ravel, Bach, Strauss, Hindemith—keep company with his beloved American ballads and spirituals.

There is something ineffably poignant about seeing this great man's clothes still hanging in the closet, protected by Pliofilm bags as if ready for their owner to return and reclaim them momentarily. Hopefully, the day will not be far away when the American public can come to him, visiting the home of this man whom President Johnson said "gave us the truest and most enduring vision of our own greatness."

The Mountains Are A-Changing

Western North Carolina with its hundreds of mountain pinnacles veiled in early morning by misty banks of clouds still has places of indescribable, almost primeval beauty. High above the valleys with their villages and patches of farm land winds the spectacular Blue Ridge Parkway. From its overlooks are vistas so magnificent they inspire a sense of awe at the vast, soaring grandeur of range after range of mountains as far as the eye can see.

Surely, a road like this could become a prototype for other parkways, not only across North Carolina but the rest of our country as well. Scenic roads for those who are eager to see beauty, quaint villages and the land itself—alternate routes to our interstates built for the traveler who is more interested in reaching his destination in a hurry. One is reminded of Robert Frost boarding his first plane who said, "May I stop and look at a flower?" Our engineers might build more roads for those who would like to stop and look at a flower, before it is too late.

In the pristine stillness of the Joyce Kilmer Memorial Forest near Robbinsville there are nature trails among gigantic oaks and hemlock trees of immense girth and dizzying heights. Streams splash, swirl and surge along, forming small waterfalls or meandering over the rocks in the sunlight. Mountain trillium blooms and ancient chestnut trees felled by a blight lie covered with emerald green moss. To see these fallen giants is almost like walking up to a dinosaur replica for the first time. The size is unbelievable. Small animals dart behind ferns and lush green ground cover, birds sing and the land is as it was a hundred years ago before the reckless, westward pillaging of man began. And so this relatively small forest will remain, because unlike our national forests, it is a memorial forest.

Nearby is Nantahala National Forest where the gods of "productivity" and "multipurpose concept" reign, allowing entire mountainsides to be clear-cut leaving only a barren, gray ridge bereft of all foliage. Seeing one of these ugly, defaced areas and

Biting its way through the mountain, these teeth cleared the right of way for Interstate 40 through the Smoky Mountains.

Under floodlights the drills work around
the clock, blasting holes and tunneling
into a mountainside for Interstate 40.
This is not a mine and it's not the Big
Ben Tunnel. It's a U. S. Interstate and
it's coming through. The mountains that
have for so long defied road builders are
finally being conquered in western North
Carolina.

The Joyce Kilmer Memorial Forest near Robbinsville was dedicated to the author of the poem Trees on the eighteenth anniversary of his death. One of the most magnificent stands of trees in America, it includes oak, hemlock and poplar as high as 125 feet and 20 feet in circumference. This virgin forest is to be maintained as primitive wilderness.

questioning why the face of the mountain is strewn with fallen trees, I am told by a young ranger, "We don't worry about that. We are trained to raise trees as a crop. Productivity is the big thing and in ten years you will see that mountainside filled with scrub growth." It does not occur to him that in ten years I don't want to look at that mountainside and see scrub growth, I want to see beauty.

"Twenty years from now those trees will be ready to harvest again. We call this multipurpose use of our national forests." The concept of multipurpose sounds so practical and innovative at first that only later does one begin to have second thoughts and question whether the fulfillment of each of man's needs is not somehow diminished. The logger's criterion for "maturity" in a tree is its having grown enough to be harvested at a profit. This means that one hundred-year-old timber might be cut, the tract reseeded and cut again in forty years, although such a short harvesting cycle can deplete soil so it will only sustain three or four generations more of trees. We are allowing cutting every twenty years!

"We also thin the forests so the trees can grow larger," the ranger continues to explain. It is amazing that the trees in this country, discovered in the 1500s, managed to attain such mammoth proportions without the help of such "judicious thinning." In Nancy Wood's Sierra Club book *Clearcut: The Deforestation of America*, she takes the forest service to task for permitting this kind of policy, as well as permitting clear-cutting itself, which makes deserts of mountains, and for approving haphazard road construction which increases erosion and downstream siltation by dangerous amounts.

She quotes a Weyerhaeuser official who says, "There is a mystique in trees, an emotional involvement as opposed to cornstalks. We must set this druidism aside and avoid emotion."

As the mountains change there are jobs for the natives, such as bulldozing for new housing developments and shopping centers, waiting table, tending bar and other service-related occupations. But the hefty profits most often go to the outsider, the wealthy entrepreneur who is able to utilize cheap labor. Highly trained, skilled labor which could be an attraction for many clean, unpolluting industries is still years away. Except for the increased flow of tax dollars that will, undoubtedly, help schools in the resort areas, little of this wealth finds its way back into the mountain coves and hollows to benefit the families who have lived there for generations.

They are descendants of predominantly Scotch-Irish settlers who first came to the mountain frontier, and have been isolated from the rest of the world by rugged mountain ranges and their own feelings of inability to cope with our society. Television has helped overcome this isolation and some have escaped—the more gifted to an education which seldom brings them back to an area still lacking any variety of opportunity, the others to large cities where without marketable skills they often merely subsist, lonely and displaced, so homesick that they sometimes drive hundreds of miles just to get home for a weekend.

A diary kept during the 1800s of an expedition to the mountains related: "Part of the way we had to crawl on hands and feet; sometimes we had to take the baggage and saddles off the horses and drag them up the mountains, for the horses were in danger of falling backwards—as we once had an experience—and sometimes we had to pull the horses up while they trembled and quivered like leaves."

It is a long way from crawling on hands and feet to the sight of tourists driving up a well-graded blacktop to a luxurious ski lodge—a long, long way. And there are many problems that must be solved if we are to preserve the beauty of the mountains and at the same time provide opportunity for the people.

Many mountaineers have kept alive the colorful customs of quilting, caning chair bottoms, wood carving, dulcimer making and fiddling, but crafts are seldom highly profitable because of the amount of time involved in handwork.

The success of a new mountain resort is small comfort to the mountaineer whose property taxes have risen to the point that he must leave the land he loves with no idea of what he will do elsewhere. Increasing numbers of tourists and tourist facilities brought problems in their wake that the more responsible leaders of the mountain counties are now realizing must be met.

Western North Carolina still reaps the bitter harvest of the time almost two decades after the Civil War when there were no schools in the mountains and three or four generations of illiterate children were the result. Today, the brightest hope of its people lies in the educational resources and talents in the mountain colleges and universities. At the same time, it will be criminal if the emphasis at these schools is on turning out more graduates in fields where the job market is already glutted. Hands that have proved adept at crafts can also be trained for highly skilled occupations—occupations

A mountain locator on the Blue Ridge Parkway helps locate mountains by name.

Church near Celo, North Carolina.

that may not necessarily fit into preconceived academic concepts but are needed in our society. For some, the answer may be university extension programs of a kind never considered before, or a relationship of co-operation between university resources and vocational schools. Our university administrations may need re-education so that they will feel neither threatened by nor superior to vocational schools but capable of an enriching, co-operative relationship. Mindless concepts of education for education's sake must give way to education for living and making relevant contributions to a rapidly changing society. If today's students are not finding today's education meaningful, the schools may be at fault.

Some universities are giving valuable assistance to their region in planning land use, zoning, air- and water-pollution control, water and sewage systems development, leisure-time activities and manpower development. If their study recommendations are acted upon by boards at the county and state level with courage and authority to enforce compliance, even when corporate pocketbooks are involved, the future of the mountains can contain both beauty and economic opportunity.

A polluted river in western North Carolina photographed several years ago.
The Air and Water Resources Board of the state is moving to eliminate such sights.

This satellite tracking station is located near Rosman, North Carolina, surrounded by
mountains, isolated from power lines, television and radio signals. With its giant antennae
the station both sends and receives satellite data for NASA.

Can We Keep the Goodliest Land?

If John Lederer, the first European to explore the Piedmont and the Blue Ridge Mountains and record his discoveries, had arrived three hundred years later he would have been in more danger quenching his thirst at a stream than he ever had been from hostile Indians. And Hernando de Soto, traveling across country, would have been astounded by the amount of metal to be found. Not gold under the ground, but shiny chrome and steel machines, row upon row of them covering the hillsides or dotting the edges of some of our roads. De Soto would certainly have been curious as to why all this metal had been abandoned.

Much has happened since the early settlers arrived in "the goodliest land."

We have cleared and scarred some of our mountainsides to get at the minerals beneath the surface, we have clear-cut timber even in our national forests. We have used our streams to carry off industrial waste as we reach out indiscriminately for more industry, and poisonous pesticides run off into them as we strive for the utmost in production from our farm lands. We have killed off the whales once plentiful off the North Carolina coasts and decimated our wild game.

However, we still have a surprising amount of our natural resources left—not because we have been cleverer or shown more foresight than other states, but simply because "progress" in the sense of industry and development has been slower in arriving here. Fortunately, we are at a point in history when we can see the effect of industrial unconcern and haphazard development in other parts of the country. The next few sessions of the North Carolina Legislature will be crucial in determining what happens here, for time is running out and the health and quality of life of all our people are at stake.

John Steinbeck has said, "No longer do we Americans want to destroy wantonly, but our new-found sources of power to take the burden of work from our shoulders, to warm us, and cool us, and give us light, to transport us quickly, and to make the things we use and wear and eat—these power sources spew pollution in our country, so that the rivers and streams are becoming poisonous and lifeless. The birds die for the lack of food; a poisonous cloud hangs over our cities that burns our lungs and reddens our eyes. Our ability to conserve has not grown with our power to create, but this slow and sullen poisoning is no longer ignored or justified. Almost daily the pressure of outrage among Americans grows. We are no longer content to destroy our beloved country . . . We are slow to learn; but we learn. . . . And we no longer believe that a man, by owning a piece of America, is free to outrage it."

Flying over the state, it is apparent that some of what Steinbeck said is already happening here. Over both mountains and cities there is more and more smog. It is increasingly difficult to photograph our changing city skylines with their new skyscrapers and show the setting sun. Our children ride city school buses through areas in which the industrial pollution causes young voices raised in song to become a chorus of coughs. Exhaust fumes from heavy automobile traffic during the morning rush hour add to the discomfort. Transportation is one of the five major causes of our air-pollution problem.

A member of our Air and Water Resources Board describes the present North Carolina environmental situation as a "mixed, murky prospect full of pluses and minuses with the future in doubt." Are we going to fall on the side of protection or exploitation? Will the money motive predominate or responsibility for the health and best interests of the public? The issue must be resolved. What sacrifices must we as North Carolinians be willing to make when it comes to our pocketbook and even our comfort if we are to insure our own health and that of our children?

City streets and highways are carrying far more than the number of vehicles for which they were originally intended, compounding congestion, pollution and human tensions. But rapid transit stays on the drawing boards because the highway construction industry, which depends on building more and more roads, opposes it. Along with industry, jets, automobiles and trucks are heavy polluters—trucking is a major North Carolina industry. But a representative of one of the larger trucking firms says, "Pollution regulation can benefit the industry. We probably get better fuel mileage by having to meet these regulations. The state has already begun to sponsor sessions for trucking firms on meeting new regulations."

However, there will be some industries which will not have quite so co-operative a response. Attitudes have not changed too much since the discovery of safety glass when the president of one of the major Detroit auto manufacturing firms said that when it came to safety glass he was primarily concerned with profits. The conflict between profit and the public interest will not be easily resolved. Companies will threaten to go out of business or tell us that tremendous price increases will have to be passed on to the public—tax credits or federal help might ease the burden for companies that do have legitimate problems. Lobbyists will be paid substantial sums to pressure our state legislators, reminding politicians that these are the companies that contribute to their campaign chests when they run for office. These company lobbyists will push for "mild" anti-pollution measures. Our answer must be—reasonable, yes; mild, no. Hopefully, there will be enough legislators with courage to stand up under pressure and, if necessary, remind some industries that a good customer is a live and healthy customer.

On the plus side of the picture, laws were passed during the recent sessions of the legislature which were an excellent beginning. One requires permits to dredge or fill the mouths of rivers emptying into the ocean or state-owned lakes. This law does not go far enough, however, for there is no protection for privately owned swamps or wetlands. We are still unable to prevent the filling in of a swamp even if it endangers the level of the water supply for an entire area, for these swamps recharge our water tables as well as provide a home for waterfowl and game for hunters.

A new Mining Act requires a permit, constant backfilling and the posting of a $25,000 bond, with the state having the right to increase the bond. In Kentucky, strip miners have found it cheaper to forfeit the bond than repair the damage, leaving vast areas of scarred mountainsides in their wake. This act is an attempt to prevent such ravaging of our mountains.

The 1971 legislature also passed an important Environmental Policy Act to govern state projects, but the next legislature must follow it up by passing laws that deal with specific environmental problems and give regulatory powers to state agencies with appropriations for monitoring and enforcement.

In two major ways the 1971 session of the legislature let the people of North Carolina down. Unlike some other states, they did not grant individual citizens the right to sue, nor did the legislature pass any laws that would help preserve open areas of farm land by easing the ever-rising tax burden of a landowner in the path of resort or commercial property. This lower tax rate could also help a historic site whose owners might suddenly find their tax rate zooming if a Holiday Inn were built beside it.

A law providing for "citizen suit" can serve three useful purposes: keeping the enforcement departments on their toes about enforcing their own standards; putting a company on notice that they must "take steps" to comply or be closed up; acting as a deterrent to companies although most citizens may never exercise the right.

Along the coast, resort developers have not always developed responsibly, particularly those who are not natives. They leave the area after their resort is completed, and there are complaints of poor sewage plants, lots that wash away and shoddy water systems. The developer has made his money as have the people who sold him the land and the local construction crews. Now it is up to the taxpayer to foot the bill for correcting the problems left behind and citizens all over the state will pay for this as they have had to do in New Jersey and the San Francisco Bay area. It is cheaper to establish standards and pay state personnel to check compliance during the construction rather than go to court later.

We must stop the sewage outflow into our sounds and rivers and treat this waste properly before putting it directly into the ocean; recycling would appear to be the best method. The alternative to sewage plants are combination sewage and water treatment plants and they must be built—with the help of federal and state funds when necessary.

The senior vice president of Public and Environmental Affairs for the American Petroleum Institute has said, "Steps to dispose of industrial, municipal, agricultural and other wastes must be achieved without cutting back on our standard of living." This sounds fine but it may not be possible. Industry may have to relinquish some of their profits and consumers may have to cut back on their standard of living and pay part of the clean-up bill. If sacrifices are called for, we must do our best to distribute the burden fairly. To operate on the theory that we will make no sacrifices for our environment is both foolhardy and dangerous.

Now, as never before, we must have co-operation among government, industry and the public if we are to preserve the natural resources of over five million North Carolinians. For none of us wants to see "evening" come to the goodliest land.